Mastering C#

Mastering Computer Science
Series Editor: Sufyan bin Uzayr

Mastering C#: A Beginner's Guide
Mohamed Musthafa MC, Divya Sachdeva, and Reza Nafim

Mastering GitHub Pages: A Beginner's Guide
Sumanna Kaul and Shahryar Raz

Mastering Unity: A Beginner's Guide
Divya Sachdeva and Aruqqa Khateib

Mastering Unreal Engine: A Beginner's Guide
Divya Sachdeva and Aruqqa Khateib

Mastering Java: A Beginner's Guide
Divya Sachdeva and Natalya Ustukpayeva

Mastering Python for Web: A Beginner's Guide
Mathew Rooney and Madina Karybzhanova

For more information about this series, please visit: https://www.routledge.com/Mastering-Computer-Science/book-series/MCS

The "Mastering Computer Science" series of books are authored by the Zeba Academy team members, led by Sufyan bin Uzayr.

Zeba Academy is an EdTech venture that develops courses and content for learners primarily in STEM fields, and offers education consulting to Universities and Institutions worldwide. For more info, please visit https://zeba.academy

Mastering C#

A Beginner's Guide

Edited by Sufyan bin Uzayr

CRC Press

Taylor & Francis Group

Boca Raton London New York

CRC Press is an imprint of the
Taylor & Francis Group, an **informa** business

First edition published 2022
by CRC Press
6000 Broken Sound Parkway NW, Suite 300, Boca Raton, FL 33487-2742

and by CRC Press
2 Park Square, Milton Park, Abingdon, Oxon, OX14 4RN

CRC Press is an imprint of Taylor & Francis Group, LLC

© 2022 Sufyan bin Uzayr

ISBN: 9781032103235 (hbk)
ISBN: 9781032103228 (pbk)
ISBN: 9781003214779 (ebk)

DOI: 10.1201/9781003214779

Typeset in Minion
by KnowledgeWorks Global Ltd.

Contents

About the Editor

Sufyan bin Uzayr is a writer, coder, and entrepreneur with more than a decade of experience in the industry. He has authored several books in the past, pertaining to a diverse range of topics, ranging from History to Computers/IT.

Sufyan is the Director of Parakozm, a multinational IT company specializing in EdTech solutions. He also runs Zeba Academy, an online learning and teaching vertical with a focus on STEM fields.

Sufyan specializes in a wide variety of technologies, such as JavaScript, Dart, WordPress, Drupal, Linux, and Python. He holds multiple degrees, including ones in Management, IT, Literature, and Political Science.

Sufyan is a digital nomad, dividing his time between four countries. He has lived and taught in universities and educational institutions around the globe. Sufyan takes a keen interest in technology, politics, literature, history and sports, and in his spare time, he enjoys teaching coding and English to young students.

Learn more at sufyanism.com.

CHAPTER 1

Mastering C# Programming Language— A Beginner's Guide

IN THIS CHAPTER

- ➢ What is C#?
- ➢ Basic Introduction to C#
- ➢ Evolution of C#

In this fast-moving world of digital transformation, almost everyone has access to the Internet and smartphones. The use of the Internet is all about browsing websites and several

DOI: 10.1201/9781003214779-1

kinds of mobile apps. Interestingly, you may not count the number of apps that you use per day. Whether it's most rampantly used microblogging apps like Twitter, streaming services like Netflix, messaging apps like WhatsApp, the coding stays at the foundation of everything. There are over 1.7 billion websites on the Internet today, all of which are powered by some programming language. It continues to evolve in both industry and research as systems and applications change. Programming is the process that makes it possible to create software, applications, and websites. It is a kind of artificial language that can be used to control the behavior of a machine, particularly a computer or other gadget like a mobile. We already know that computers or any other similar technologies cannot think themselves; they require users to give sets of ordered instructions to know what to do. So programming works here. It is used to facilitate communication about organizing and manipulating information and express algorithms precisely. Its languages are entirely different from most other forms of human expression in that they require a greater degree of precision and completeness.

This sort of language is referred to as "code." Most of the resources you use on the computer and Internet are made with code. Learning this sort of coding is simple. All you need is some idea and the right tool. Coding an app involves taking a picture, designing the app, testing it, and releasing it. There is never a better ideal time to develop an app than today. Surprisingly, you have an enormous market for your app once it hits Google Play and App Store. If you are newer to the mobile app development world but ardently want to be part of it somehow by yourself, this book is a detailed guide that will help learners get started with C# programming. It firstly talks about the basics and then moves on to practical exercises to help readers quickly gain the required knowledge.

INTRODUCTION TO C# PROGRAMMING LANGUAGE

C# is a general-purpose, advanced and Object-Oriented Programming Language pronounced as "C sharp" created by Microsoft that runs on the .NET Framework. C# has roots in the C family, and the language is close to other popular languages like C++ and Java. The first version was released in the year 2002. The latest version, C# 8, was released in September 2019. C# is recognized as a standard by ECMA and ISO. C# is specifically designed for Common Language Infrastructure (CLI). It's a standard for describing executable code and the environment in which it runs. C# was initially known as C-like Object-Oriented Language (COOL) but altered the name to prevent trademark concerns. Since the C# is formed within the .Net Framework initiative by Microsoft, it provides various integrated development environments (IDEs) to run C# programs smoothly.

While C# can be put to better use in the hands of all sorts of programmers, a large part of the language's user base comprises those who are partial to the Microsoft platform.

WHAT IS C#

C# (pronounced "C-sharp") is an object-based programming language from Microsoft that significantly focuses on combining the computing power of C++ with the programming ease of Visual Basic. C# is based on C++ and includes features similar to those of Java. It's a blend between C and C++. C# is commonly used for backend services, windows applications, website development, and game development.

C# is arranged to work with Microsoft's .NET platform. Microsoft's main aim is to facilitate exchanging information and services over the web and let developers build highly portable applications. C# smoothen programming by using Extensible Markup Language (XML) and Simple Object Access Protocol (SOAP), which allowed access to a programming object or method without requiring the programmer to write additional code for each step. That is something quite interesting. Do you know one thing? Programmers here can build on existing code rather than repeatedly duplicating it. C# is expected to make it faster and less expensive to market new products and services. C# programs run on .NET and a virtual execution system called the common language runtime (CLR) and included many class libraries. The CLR is the implementation of the CLI by Microsoft, an international standard. The CLI is the ground for creating execution and development environments in which languages and libraries work together continuously.

Source code written in C# is compiled into an intermediate language (IL) that matches the CLI specification. The IL code and its resources, like bitmaps and strings, are saved in an assembly, which usually ends in.dll. A pack includes a manifest that provides information about the assembly's types, genre, and culture.

When the C# program is carried out, the assembly is filled into the CLR. The CLR performs Just-In-Time (JIT) compilation to change the IL code to native machine instructions. The CLR gives other services related to automatic garbage collection, exception handling, and resource management. Code carried out by the CLR is sometimes referred to as "managed code," in comparison with "unmanaged code," which is composed into native machine language that selects a specific platform.

Language interoperability is a crucial feature .NET. IL code produced by the C# compiler conforms to the Common Type Specification (CTS). IL code generated from C# can simply interact with code generated from the .NET versions of F#, Visual Basic, C++, or any of more than 20 other CTS-compliant languages. A single assembly may include different modules written in different .NET languages, and the types can reference each other as if they were written in the same, unique language.

Besides the runtime services, .NET also includes comprehensive libraries. These libraries support many different kinds of workloads. They're organized into namespaces that give a wide variety of proper functionality for everything from file input and output to string manipulation to XML parsing, web application frameworks, and Windows Forms controls. The typical C# application utilizes the .NET class library considerably to handle every day "plumbing" chores.

WHY C# MATTERS

As a beginner, it's pretty simple to learn C#; to know C#, you should have at least a basic idea of writing code, even if you have yet to build your first application or program. The learning curve for C# is comparatively low when compared to more complex languages.

C# is an excellent choice for developers with moderate to advanced experience with writing code. While experts admit the language is one of the reasonable complexities, they agree that it's relatively simple to grasp and outperform. Once you're introduced to C# and put in the time to get the hang of it, you can expect to advance quickly from an amateur to an expert.

This is since C# is a first-class language, which means it's relatably easy to grasp and write, making it a splendid choice for beginners and a convenient option for experts. In addition to readability, C# can also automate complex tasks that require a lot of time to achieve minor results.

This programming language is also statistically typed, which means that errors are identified before the application goes live. This makes it simple to detect minor flaws in your stack that would otherwise be almost.

HISTORY OF C#

In 2000, Microsoft announced its initial version of C# as a part of the .NET Framework. VB.NET was also an alternative, but VB.NET stuck to the standard Microsoft Visual Basic syntax, while C# was close to Java, a C-style language. The name was given to C# firstly was "Cool." Microsoft was conscious of working with a language very approximately to C++, so they wanted to specify that its new language was one step higher than C++. C# is a newly discovered language on the market developed by Microsoft. Initially, Microsoft advanced and deployed the

Active Server Pages (ASP) language. This language is now labeled Classic ASP, and its support has been discontinued. ASP lets programmers generate VB-like scripts to enlarge dynamic web pages. These sort of web pages continued on aged Internet information Services (IIS) servers running Windows. Some Linux providers also supported Classic ASP, but it was routinely a nonstandard way to create web pages. In the late 1990s, Microsoft decided to make a language that fought a tight-spirited fight with Java. During this course of time, Java was the most common language, and its popularity was rising. Classic ASP had its place, but the software required to create the product was a paid application. Java was used to develop web applications, and it was favored among developers who understood C and C++. Instead of label the new language C+++, they decided to use the name C# (pronounced C sharp), which attributes the musical notation that a note should be higher in pitch. The C# team is continuing to innovate and add new specific features.

This chapter provides a history of a significant release of the C# language as they are meticulously focusing on remarkable innovation and adding spectacular features to this.

- C# version 1.0.

- C# version 1.2.

- C# version 2.0.

- C# version 3.0.

- C# version 4.0.

- C# version 5.0.

- C# version 6.0.

- C# version 7.0.

- C# version 7.1.

- C# version 7.2.

- C# version 7.3.

- C# version 8.0.

- C# version 9.0.

C# Version 1.0

Microsoft released the first version of C# with Visual Studio 2002. Use of managed code was introduced with this version. C# 1.0 was the first language that developers adopted to build .NET applications.

The significant features of C# 1.0 include:

- Classes.

- Structs.

- Interfaces.

- Events.

- Properties.

- Delegates.

C# Version 1.2

This version was introduced with Visual Studio .NET 2003. It mainly includes a few minor enhancements to the language. The most significant is that the code generated a for each loop called Dispose on an IEnumerator when IEnumerator implemented IDisposable.

C# Version 2.0

With Visual Studio 2005 (formerly codenamed Whidbey), C# is back with some innovations. The C# language has successfully been updated to version 2.0 and comes with several language extensions. Besides generic types, the C# language introduces other exciting features such as Iterators, Partial Classes, Anonymous methods, partial types, and Nullable value types.

Other C# 2.0 features essentially added capabilities to existing features:

- Getter/setter separate accessibility.

- Method group conversions (delegates).

- Static classes.

- Delegate inference.

While C# may have started as a generic OOL, C# version 2.0 changed that hastily. Once they had complete control over them, they went after some complicated developer pain points. And they even went after them in a significant way.

C# Version 3.0

C# version 3.0 was released as part of .Net version 3.5. Many of the features added explicitly with this version supported Language Integrated Queries (LINQ).

List of added features:

- LINQ.

- Lambda expressions.

- Extension methods.

- Anonymous types.

- Implicitly typed variables.

- Object and collection initializers.

- Automatically implemented properties.

- Expression trees.

In retrospect, many of these features above seem both inevitable and inseparable. They all fit together strategically. It's generally thought that the C# version's killer feature was the query expression, also popularly known as Language-Integrated Query (LINQ).

A more nuanced view examines expression trees, lambda expressions, and anonymous types as the foundation of LINQ. But, in either case, C# 3.0 introduced a breathtaking concept. C# 3.0 had begun to lay the groundwork for turning C# into a hybrid OOL/Functional language. Importantly, you could now write SQL-style declarative queries to perform operations on collections, among other things.

C# Version 4.0

Microsoft introduced this version of the C# in April 2010 with Visual Studio 2010. Mono C# compiler fully supported the new version by October 2010 with the release of

Mono 2.8. The next version did introduce some interesting new features:

- Dynamic binding
- Named/optional arguments
- Generic covariant and contravariant
- Embedded interop types

The new version of the C# language brought a new type of dynamic. Once a variable is declared as having type dynamic, operations on these values are not done or verified at compile-time but instead happen entirely at run-time. This is also known as duck typing.

Embedded interop types eased the deployment pain of creating COM interop assemblies for your application. Generic and contravariance provide you with more power to use generics, but they're a bit academic and probably most appreciated by framework and library authors. Named and optional parameters let you eliminate many method overloads and provide convenience. But none of those features are precisely paradigm-altering.

C# Version 5.0

C# version 5.0, released with Visual Studio 2012, was a focused version of the language. Almost all of the effort for that version went into another disruptive language concept: the async and await model for asynchronous programming. Here's the list of the significant features:

- Asynchronous methods.
- Caller info attributes.

The Async feature establishes two keywords, async and await, which allows you to write asynchronous code more quickly and intuitively like synchronous code. Before C# 5.0, for writing an asynchronous code, you have to define callbacks (also known as continuations) to capture what happens after an asynchronous process completes. This makes your code and another routine task such as exception handling complicated. Caller information can help you out in tracing, debugging, and creating diagnosis tools. It will help you avoid duplicate codes that are generally invoked in many methods for the same purpose, such as logging and tracing.

C# Version 6.0

With versions 3.0 and 5.0, C# had added significant and outstanding new features in an OOL. With unique version 6.0, released with Visual Studio 2015, it would wane from doing a dominant killer feature and, in lieu, release many more minor features that made C# programming more productive. The C# 6.0 version contains many essential elements which will improve the productivity of developers. Here are some of them:

- Using static.

- Exception filters.

- Auto-property initializers.

- Expression bodied members.

- Null propagator.

- String interpolation.

- Name of operator.

- Index initializers.

- Await in catch/finally blocks.

- Default values for getter-only properties.

Each of these features is quite interesting in its own right. But if you gaze at them all together, you see an interesting pattern. In this version, C# eliminated language boilerplate to make code more terse and readable. So for fans of clean, simple code, this language version was a huge win.

C# Version 7.0

With Visual Studio 2017 (March 7, 2017), we got a new version of C#—C# 7.0. There is a lot of new exciting features that nicely build on top of existing ones.

Here is an overview of new features in C#:

- Out variables.

- Pattern matching.

- Tuples.

- Deconstruction.

- Discards.

- Local functions.

- Binary literals.

- Digit separators.

All of these features provide extraordinary new capabilities for developers and the opportunity to write even cleaner code than ever. A highlight is condensing the declaration of variables to use with the out keyword and allowing multiple return values via tuple.

But C# is being put to ever broader use. .NET Core now targets any operating system and has its eyes firmly on the cloud and portability. These new capabilities indeed occupy the language designers' thoughts and time and come up with new features.

C# Version 7.1

C# 7.1 was released in August 2017 as part of the 15.3 updates for Visual Studio 2017. The most notable new feature in C# 7.1 is the ability to have an async Main method. With C# 7.0, we started seeing point releases on C#, starting with version 7.1. This marked an increased·release cadence for C#. New language features for this release were:

- Async Main method,

- Default literal expressions,

- Inferred tuple element names, and

- Pattern matching on generic type parameters.

C# 7.1 also added the language version selection configuration element, as well as new compiler behavior.

C# Version 7.2

C# 7.2 added a few more minor language features to C#. These were:

- The addition of code enhancements allowing developers to write safe, efficient code,

- The in modifier on parameters,

- The ref read-only modifier on method returns,

- The read-only struct declaration,

- The ref struct declaration,

- Non-trailing named arguments,

- Leading underscores in numeric literals,

- Private protected access modifier, and

- Conditional ref expressions.

C# Version 7.3

The point releases of C# 7 allowed developers to get their hands on new language features sooner rather than later. It was the release of C# 7.3 that had two main themes. One theme allowed safe code to perform unsafe code, and the other provided additional improvements to existing features.

From a better performant, safe code perspective, we saw:

- The accessing of fields without pinning;

- Reassigning ref local variables;

- On stackalloc arrays, initializers are used;

- Fix statements can be used with any type that supports a pattern; and

- Additional generic constraints.

C# Version 8.0

C# 8.0 is the first major C# release that explicitly targets
.NET Core. Some features rely on new CLR capabilities,
others on library types added only in .NET Core. C# 8.0
added up the following specifications and enhancements
to the C# language:

- Default interface methods.

- Nullable reference types.

- Pattern matching enhancements.

- Asynchronous streams/Asynchronous disposable.

- Using declarations.

- Enhancement of interpolated verbatim strings.

- Null-coalescing assignment.

- Static local functions.

- Indices and ranges.

- Unmanaged constructed types.

- Read-only member.

Nullable reference types are perhaps the most significant
feature in C# 8.0. It introduces a configurable change
whereby reference types are non-nullable by default but
can explicitly allow null with a nullable modifier. Of
course, the new feature list doesn't stop there. Other more
prominent features include support for data and pattern
matching improvements. The latter provides a terse syntax

instead of switch expressions (yes, expressions) that enable conditional checks to evaluate the shape and data within an object to determine a result. In addition, there are several miscellaneous enhancements such as default interface implementations, using declarations, static local functions, indices/ranges, and a null-coalescing assignment operator.

C# Version 9.0

C# 9.0 was released with .NET 5. It's the default language version for any assembly that targets the .NET 5 release. Many C# 9.0 features rely on new features in the .NET 5.0 libraries and updates to the .NET CLR that's part of .NET 5.0. Therefore, C# 9.0 is supported only on .NET 5.0. C# 9.0 focuses on features that help native cloud applications, modern software engineering practices, and more concise readable code.

C# 9.0 adds the following features and enhancements to the C# language:

- Top-level statements.

- Record types.

- Init-only setters.

- Enhancements to pattern matching.

- Natural-sized integers.

- Function pointers.

- Omit localsinit.

- Target type new.

- Target type conditional.

- Static anonymous methods.

- Covariant return types.

- Lambda discard parameters.

- Attributes on local functions.

C# 9.0 continues three themes from previous releases: removing ceremony, separating data from algorithms, and providing more patterns in more places. The introduction of the record offers a concise syntax for reference types that follow value semantics for equality. You'll use these types to define data containers that typically define minimal behavior. Init-only setters provide the capability for the nondestructive mutation (with expressions) in records. C# 9.0 also adds covariant return types so that derived forms can override virtual methods and return a style derived from the base method's return type.

UNDERSTANDING THE BASIC STRUCTURE OF THE C# PROGRAM

A typical C# program includes several different parts as shown below:

- Namespace.

- Class.

- The main method.

- Methods inside the class.

- Class definition or class attributes.

- Statements.

- Comments.

Few things need to be kept in your mind while writing a C# program. C# programs are case-sensitive, which does mean "string" is different from "String." All the statements you write in the program should be concluded with a semi-colon, i.e., ";" a semicolon tells the program explicitly that the current line of the statement has ended.

USING KEYWORD

The using keyword is importantly used to handle any object used to carry out the namespace. It is mainly used to bring in a namespace. Because a namespace is a collection of classes, each of which has its functionality, we can use the keyword to implement various features from the namespace that has been imported.

NAMESPACE

A namespace is a logical grouping of similar classes and objects. Its purpose is to keep a diverse group of items apart from one another. This allows programmers to define one class in one namespace and another in a different namespace without generating any problems.

Let's pretend we're creating two namespaces: "fruits" and "colors." Both of these namespaces can have an "Orange" class without interfering with any other. A namespace is created by entering the name of the namespace followed by the term namespace.

Namespace ConsoleApplication, for example.

CLASS

Defining a class is analogous to defining a data type's blueprint. The data is not described by style; instead, it is organized as a significant entity.

For instance, if we have a class called "Fruit," we may create many related objects within it, such as mango, apple, grapes, and so on. Thus, the class fruit will contain different objects with other properties such as color, smell, taste edible, etc. Each of these items and property will be a part of the class.

Similar to the example mentioned above, the Object-Oriented Programming Language such as C# also defines different properties inside, i.e., fields, methods, conditions, events, etc. The objects inside the class include a definition of the operations that can be performed. Objects are an instance of the class and the methods or the variables that are the class members. In summary, the course enables you to create unique objects by combining different techniques, events, and object kinds.

A class is defined by preceding the course name with the keyword "class." A pair of curly braces determine the class body.

```
class program1
{
//body
of the class
}
```

Access Modifiers

It defines the accessibility of an object, and it is very components. All C# components have an access level that may be controlled using access modifiers to restrict access to member objects inside the class.

To define the accessibility level of the object, we have got to declare it by using one of the keywords provided by C# language, i.e., Public, Private, Protected, and Internal. Access modifier is expressed by using either of the keywords mentioned above before the class or a method. Example:

```
public class program//Set the access
modifier
to public.
{
}
```

METHOD

It is a collection of statements that work together to complete a job. At least one class with one Main method will be present in every C# application.

It includes the following definition. It starts with an access modifier declaration, then a return type, and later, we define the method name, and inside the round bracket, we have the parameters specified.

```
{Access Modifiers} {return type definition}
Method Name({parameter})
public static void Main(String[] args){
}
```

After the method has been defined, commands or statements can be written within the curly braces. Arguments can be passed within the round bracket just after the method name.

These arguments are helpful while calling a method with specific parameters. In the above example, we have crossed only one parameter, "args," with the argument type as an array of strings.

CONSTRUCTOR

Constructors are the unique class methods that are automatically invoked whenever an instance of a specific type is created. The main advantage of the constructor is that it can initialize the private fields of a class. A class can have some constructors, and it doesn't need to have any return type.

Only one static constructor is allowed inside a class, and that cannot be parameterized. Constructors are declared by using any access modifier and then using the class name in which it is created. For Example, a constructor definition will look something like this.

```
class program1
{
public class(){ //This is a constructor
}
}
```

DATA TYPES

Data types are used in almost all programming languages. A data type tells the compiler what kind of value a variable will hold. C# has several built-in data types such as String, Integer, Float, Boolean, etc. Each data type has its own set of definitions for the values it can hold.

A data type is used to declare a variable by the primary variable with the data type keyword.

```
class program1
{
static void Main(string[] args)
    {
string stringValue = "Hello";
int integerValue = 10;
float floatValue = 13.2f;
bool booleanValue = false;
    }
}
```

CURLY BRACES

It defines the beginning and the end of any logical statement in a program block. The curly braces are restricted to the C# language, but they are also found in several other languages like Java, C++, etc. You can see our first "Hello World" code used to wrap multiple lines of code together. It marks the starting and the end point of the logical statement for the compiler.

Any logical entity like Namespace, Class, Method, Conditional statement, Loops, etc., should be enclosed inside braces to mark the start and end of the report for the compiler. For a better grasp of the overall structure of a C# program, below is the simplest C# program:

```
* C# Program Structure - Example */
using System;
namespace HelloEveryoneApp
{
   class HelloEveryoneClass
   {
      static void Main(string[] args)
      {
```

```
        /* this is first program in C#
language */
        Console.WriteLine("Hello Everyone");
        Console.ReadKey();
    }
}
```

When the above code is compiled and executed, it will produce the following output:

- Hello Everyone

Here is the explanation of the above C# program:

- **/* C# Program Structure - Example program */:** The C# compiler ignores this line; this is the comment in the program.

- **using System;:** The using keyword includes the system namespace in the C# program.

- **namespace HelloEveryoneApp:** This is the namespace declaration. It is simply a collection of classes. The HelloEveryoneApp namespace contains the class named HelloEveryoneClassclass—Here, the class HelloEveryoneClass includes the data and the method definitions that your C# program uses.

- **static void Main(string[] args):** This line defined the Main method, which is the entry point for all the C# programs.

- ***/:** The C# compiler also ignores this line; this is also a comment in the program.

- **Console.WriteLine("Hello Everyone");:** This is the same behavior of the Main method. Here the **WriteLine()** is the method of the Console class, which is defined in the system namespace. This statement causes the message **"Hello Everyone"** to be displayed on the output screen.

- **Console.ReadKey();:** This is for the VS.NET users. This statement makes the C# program wait for a keypress, and it prevents the sudden closing of the output screen when the program is launched from the Visual Studio .NET.

To compile and to run the above C# program using Visual Studio.NET (VS.NET), follow these steps:

- open visual studio

- on the menu bar

- choose FILE -> NEW -> PROJECT

- choose visual C# from templates

- choose windows

- choose console application

- specify a name for your project

- Click OK

After processing the above-given steps, your new project in the Solution Explorer is created. Now just write the above code in the Code Editor. After writing the code, to run your C# program, just press the F5 key or click on the RUN button to execute the project. After performing this, a command prompt window will appear, containing the line, Hello World.

CHAPTER 2

Building Blocks of C#

IN THIS CHAPTER

- ➢ Building Blocks of C#

- ➢ Understanding the CLI

- ➢ Methods and Operators

We learned about the basic notion of C# programming in the previous chapter, and now we'll study the building blocks of C#.

MEMBERS

The members of a class are of two types.

1. **Static members:** Static members belong to classes.

2. **Instance members:** Instance members allied to objects (instances of classes).

DOI: 10.1201/9781003214779-2

The following is the outline for the kinds of members a class can contain:

- **Fields:** Variables that are related to the class.

- **Types:** Nested types declared by the class.

- **Properties:** Actions related to reading and writing named properties of the class.

- **Constants:** Constant values associated with the class.

- **Indexers:** Actions related to indexing instances of the class like an array.

- **Events:** Notifications that the class can create.

- **Operators:** Conversions and expression operators aided by the class.

- **Constructors:** Actions need to initialize instances of the class or the class itself.

- **Methods:** Actions that the class can simply perform.

- **Finalizers:** Actions taken before the permanent deletion of instances of the class.

Accessibility

Each class member has associated accessibility, which controls the regions of program text that can access the member.

Six forms of possible accessibility can be summarised as below:

1. **Protected:** Access is confined to this class or classes derived from this class.

2. **Private protected:** Access is confined to this class or classes derived from this type within the same assembly.

3. **Protected internal:** Access is confined to this class, classes derived from this class, or classes within the same assembly.

4. **Public:** Access isn't limited.

5. **Private:** Access is limited to this class.

6. **Internal:** Access is confined to the current assembly.

Fields

A field is a variable that is related to a class or with an instance of a class.

A field stated with the static modifier expounds a static field. It precisely identifies one storage location. It is not a problem how many instances of classes are created. Only one copy of a static field would be there.

A field announced without the static modifier clearly defines an instance field. Every instance of a class includes a separate copy of all the instance fields of that class.

Methods

A method is a member that introduces a computation or action that an object or class can perform. Static methods are acquired through the class while instance methods are acquired through instances of the class.

Methods may have a bunch of parameters, which includes values or variable references given to the technique. Methods have a return type, which describes the type of the value computed and returned by the method. A method's return type is invalid if it doesn't return a value.

Like types, methods may also have many parameters, for which type arguments must be emphasized when the method is called. Unlike types, the type arguments can be understood from the arguments of a method call and need not be given.

The signature of a method should be unique in the class in which the method is declared. The signature of a method always includes the name of the method, the number of type parameters, and the modifiers, number, and types of its parameters. The signature of a method doesn't contain the return type.[1]

Parameters

Parameters are typically used to pass values or variable references to methods. The parameters of a method get their exact values from the arguments specified when the method is invoked. There are four kinds of parameters:

1. Value parameters.

2. Reference parameters.

3. Output parameters.

4. Parameter arrays.

Method Body and Local Variables

The body of a method highlights the statements that should be executed whenever the method is called.

---

[1] Bill Wagner and Aren Windham (2021).Program building blocks.*Microsoft*

Variables unique to the method invocation can be declared in the method body. It is called local variables. A local variable declaration specifies a variable name, a type name, and possibly an initial value.

Static and Instance Methods

A static method is a kind of method declared with a static modifier. It can only directly access static members and can't operate on a specific instance.

An instance method is a method declared without a static modifier. It runs on a specific instance and can easily acquire both static and instance members. The example on which an instance method was invoked can be accessed like this. It's a mistake to refer to this in a static method.

Method Overloading

Because of method overloading, various methods in the same class can have the same name as long as their signatures are distinct. The compiler uses overload resolution to find the exact method to invoke when compiling an invocation of an overloaded method. Overload resolution finds the one method that appropriately suits the arguments. An error will be reported if no single best match can be found.

The following example indicates overload resolution in effect. The comment for each of the invocations in the UsageExample method invokes which method is invoked.

MethodOverloadingExample

```
{
    static void F() => Console.
WriteLine("F()");
    static void F(object x) => Console.
WriteLine("F(object)");
    static void F(int x) => Console.
WriteLine("F(int)");
    static void F(double x) => Console.
WriteLine("F(double)");
    static void F<T>(T x) => Console.
WriteLine("F<T>(T)");
    static void F(double x, double y) =>
Console.WriteLine("F(double, double)");

    public static void UsageExample()
    {
        F();                // Invokes F()
        F(1);               // Invokes F(int)
        F(1.0);             // Invokes F(double)
        F("abc");           // Invokes
F<string>(string)
        F((double)1);       // Invokes F(double)
        F((object)1);       // Invokes F(object)
        F<int>(1);          // Invokes
F<int>(int)
        F(1, 1);            // Invokes
F(double, double)
    }
}
```

The examples above explicitly show that a particular method can always be selected by casting the same parameter types and type arguments.

Other Function Members

Members that include executable code are collectively known as the function members of a class.

Constructors

C# supports both instance and static constructors.

- **Instance constructor:** a member that implements the actions required to initialize an instance of a class.

- **Static constructor:** a member that carries out the actions needs to initialize a class itself when it's first loaded.

A constructor is announced like a method with no return type and the same name as the containing class. If a constructor declaration contains a static modifier, it declares a static constructor. If this is not the case, an instance constructor is declared.

Instance constructors can be overloaded and can have optional parameters. For example, the MyList<T> class declares one instance constructor with a single optional int parameter. Instance constructors are invoked using the new operator. The following statements allocate two MyList<string> instances using the constructor of the MyList class with and without the optional argument.

```
MyList<string> list1 = new MyList<string>();
MyList<string> list2 = new MyList<string>(10);
```

Instance constructors aren't inherited like any other members. Other than the constructors stated in the class, there are no instance constructors in a class. If a class doesn't have an instance constructor, it defaults to an empty one with no parameters.

Events

An event is a member that allows a class or object to furnish notifications. An event is stated like a field except that the declaration co an event keyword, and the type must be a delegate type.

Operators

A member that provides the meaning of applying a particular expression operator to instances of a class is called an operator. Unary operators, binary operators, and conversion operators are the three types of operators that may be specified. Public and static operators should be indicated for all operators.

Finalizers

A finalizer is a class member that implements the operations required to close a class instance. Typically, a finalizer is necessary to release unmanaged resources. Finalizers can't have parameters, they can't have accessibility modifiers, and they can't be invoked. The finalizer, for instance, is gathered automatically during garbage collection.

Expressions

Expressions are developed from operands and operators. The operators of an expression point out which operations to apply to the operands. Examples of operators include +, -, *,/, and new. Examples of operands contain literals, fields, local variables, and expressions.

Statements

The actions of a program are demonstrated using statements. C# supports different kinds of statements, several of which are defined in terms of embedded statements.

UNDERSTANDING THE CLI

The common language runtime (CLR) code uses a standard common type system (CTS) based on a common language infrastructure (CLI). CLI is part of Microsoft's .NET platform and is expected to become an ECMA standard. The CLI includes the CTS and Common Language Specification (CLS).

CLI is a specification created by Microsoft that explains the executable code and runtime environment. In simple terms, this provides us to use various high-level programming languages on numerous machines without rewriting the code.

The .NET Framework, .NET Core, and Mono are some implementations of CLI (picture).

CLI can be divided into four main components.

Common Type System

CTS is accountable for lay-outing the framework to use two or more languages simultaneously. It defines how types are declared and controlled in a source code of any .NET language in the CLR where your bytecode or portable execution file changes into machine code. It also gives the object-oriented programming (OOPs) model, which enables the execution of different high-level languages. It defines instructions that must be followed so that other languages can communicate and provide primitive data type libraries.

Common Language Specification

CLS is a set of requirements that must be met by any language for it to be considered .NET compatible. It's a collection of rules and a subset of CTS kinds. Elimination of pointers and multiple inheritances are examples of it.

Metadata

Metadata provides information about all the classes and the class members specified in the assembly.

Virtual Execution System

Virtual execution system (VES) loads and runs the programs that are compatible with the CLI.

CLI advantages are as follows:

- Defines a consistent programming model. For example, a .NET program is syntactically similar to C.NET or VB.NET and follows the same essential steps when accessing and obtaining data.

- Administrators may define and reinforce security by limiting data access and ensuring user authenticity.

- Implements protocols like HTTP, Transmission Control Protocol/Internet Protocol (TCP/IP), Simple Object Access Protocol (SOAP), and Extensible Markup Language (XML), providing technology compatibility with added security layers.

- Allows users to separate application presentation logic and business logic for increased maintenance and portability using metadata. To make it crystal clear, CLI is a bunch of specifications for a virtual operating system (OS) that is solely a CLR.

THE .NET FRAMEWORKS

NET framework is a managed execution condition for Windows that gives various services to its running apps. There are two kinds of main components of .NET Frameworks.

CLR

It is the primary and Virtual Machine component of the .NET Framework. The runtime environment in the .NET Framework runs the codes and makes the development process easier by providing various services such as remoting, thread management, type-safety, memory management, robustness, etc. It is accountable for controlling the execution of .NET programs without considering any .NET programming language. It also allows in the direction of code, as code that hit the runtime is explicitly known as the Managed Code, and code that doesn't switch to runtime is called Unmanaged code.

Framework Class Library (FCL)

The group of repeatable, object-oriented class libraries and methods, etc., can be combined with CLR. It is also called the Assemblies. It is like the header files in C/C++ and packages in java. Installing the .NET framework is the installation of CLR and FCL into the system.

App Models

The common app models for creating software applications in the .NET Framework contain the following:

- **ADO.NET:** This is always used to create applications that interact with databases, like the Microsoft SQL Server and Oracle.

- **ASP.NET:** This model is used to build web-based applications that can run on browsers.

- **WinForms:** This model is used to build forms-based applications deployed on end-user devices.

The following are some of the benefits that the NET framework provides to running apps:

- **Memory management:** Programmers are responsible for allocating and releasing memory and managing object lifetimes in many programming languages. The CLR provides various services on behalf of the app in .NET Framework applications.

- **A typical type system is as follows:** Basic types are interpreted by the compiler in conventional programming languages, complicating cross-language compatibility. In .NET Framework, basic types are determined by the .NET Framework type system and are customary to all languages that specifically target .NET Framework.

- **An extensive class library:** Programmers can use a readily accessible library of types and members from the .NET FCL instead of writing a bulk code to handle common low-level programming operations.

- **Development frameworks and technologies:** .NET Framework contains libraries for specific areas of app development, such as Windows Communication Foundation for service-oriented apps, ASP.NET for web apps, ADO.NET for data access, and Windows Presentation Foundation for Windows desktop applications.

Why Do Companies Use .NET?
Language interoperability. Language compilers that specifically target the .NET Framework release an intermediate code called Common Intermediate Language (CIL), which, in turn, is compiled at runtime by the CLR. With this, routines written in one language are available to other languages, and programmers develop apps in their preferred languages.

- **Version compatibility:** Apps created using a particular version of the .NET Framework run with no modification on a later version.

- **Side-by-side execution:** .NET Framework allows us to resolve version conflicts by letting different versions of the CLR exist on the same computer. This does mean that multiple versions of apps can simply coexist and that an app can operate on the version of the .NET Framework with which it was developed. The .NET Framework version groups are affected by side-by-side execution.

- **Multitargeting:** By hitting .NET Standard, developers built class libraries that run on multiple .NET Framework platforms supported by that standard version. Libraries targeting .NET Standard 2.0, for example, may be utilized by programs targeting the .NET Framework 4.6.1, .NET Core 2.0 and UWP 10.0.16299.

- **Reliability:** NET has been used to create and run thousands of applications since its release in 2002. Despite the creation of new and advanced versions, the earlier renditions still provide reliable performance.

- **Portability:** The .NET Framework allows applications to run on any Windows platform. It also offers cross-platform features, letting developers create programs that can operate on other OSs. Third parties can use conforming languages to create compatible framework implementations on various platforms.

- **Integrates with legacy systems:** The .NET Framework can integrate with legacy systems such as XML smoothly. It can quickly write and process any file format, making it a flexible system with several uses.

.NET Framework for Users

If you don't create .NET Framework apps but use them, you don't need to have a specific understanding of the .NET Framework or its operation. In most cases, the framework is fully transparent to users.

If Windows is your OS, .NET Framework may already be installed on your computer. Not only that, if you install an app that needs .NET Framework, the app's setup program itself might install a specific version of the framework on your computer. You may notice a dialog box that asks you to install .NET Framework in some cases. If you've just tried to operate an app when this dialog box pop up and if your computer has Internet availability, you can go to a webpage that lets you install the missing version of the .NET Framework.

In general, you should not uninstall .NET Framework versions that are already installed on your machine for two reasons:

If you utilize an app that relies on a specific version of the .NET Framework, it may stop working if that version is removed.

Some versions of the .NET Framework are in-place updates to earlier versions. For example, .NET Framework 3.5 is an in-place update to version 2.0, and .NET Framework 4.8 updates versions 4 through 4.7.2.

On Windows 8, if you choose to delete .NET Framework, always use Programs and Features from Control Panel to uninstall it. Never delete a version of the .NET Framework manually. On Windows 8 and above, .NET Framework is an OS component and is impossible to be independently uninstalled.

Multiple versions of the .NET Framework can coexist on a single computer simultaneously. This means you won't have to uninstall prior versions before installing the new one.

If it's not installed on your OS earlier, then install the version of the .NET Framework that your app will target. The new version is .NET Framework 4.8. It is already installed on Windows post May 10, 2019 Update and subsequent updates, and now it's available for download on earlier versions of the Windows OS. Additional .NET Framework packages are released out of band, which means they're released on a rolling basis outside of any regular or scheduled release cycle.

Select and install the development environment to develop your apps, which helps your selected programming language or languages. The Microsoft integrated development environment (IDE) for .NET Framework apps in Visual Studio. It's available in several editions. The combination of OS Architecture and CPU Architecture is known as the platform. Platform dependent means the programming language code will work only on a particular OS. A .NET application is platform-dependent because of the .NET framework, which operates only on the Windows-based OS. The .NET application is also platform-independent because of the Mono framework. Using the Mono framework, the .NET application can work on any OS, including windows.

Important Points

NET for Visual Studio is the development tool that is used to design and create .NET applications. For using Visual Studio, the user first need to install the .NET framework on the computer.

In the earlier version of Windows OS like XP SP1, SP2, or SP3, the .NET framework was integrated with the installation media.

Windows 8, 8.1, or 10 do not provide an already installed version 3.5 or later of the .NET Framework. So, it is crucial for a version higher than 3.5 must be installed either from a Windows installation media or from the Internet on demand. Windows update will recommend installing the .NET framework.work, which can only run on the Windows-based OS. The .NET application is also platform-independent because of the Mono framework. By using the Mono framework, the .NET application can run on any OS, including windows.

What Languages Do Developers Have
Access to While Working with .NET?
The .NET Framework is a multi-language framework that allows for interoperability between supported programming languages. The framework supports these programming languages:

- **C#:** This is an advanced, OOPs language that gives garbage collection, versioning type-safety, scalability support, and other productivity-increasing features. It's easy to use and can help you save time while developing apps.

- **F#:** This is a cross-platform, open-source language with excellent OOPs features. It is a primary functional programming language .NET.

- **Visual Basic:** It is a simple language used to develop object-oriented apps. It provides type safety and uses simple syntax.

Developers can use managed C++, IronPython, Visual COBOL, IronRuby, and many other languages found in the Visual Studio Languages to code in .NET.

To create .NET apps or components, follow these steps:

- Install the .NET Framework version that will be used to execute your application.

- Select the .NET Framework language that you'll use to build your project. C#, F#, C++, Visual Basic, and IronRuby are all options.

- Select and install a development environment that will allow you to construct compatible applications. Microsoft Visual Studio is the IDE for the .NET Framework.

ASSEMBLIES IN .NET

The primary building block in the Assembly. Applications that use the .NET Framework. It is a compiled code that the CLR can simply execute. It is a collection of resources and types created to work together and build a logical base of functionality. It can be a DLL or exe based upon the project that we choose. You may create an assembly from one or more source code files in .NET Core and .NET Framework. In .NET Framework, assemblies can include one or more modules. This provides larger projects to be designed so that other developers can work on different source code files or modules, which are incorporated to build a single assembly. Assemblies are essentially the building blocks of .NET Framework applications. Metadata is created with Microsoft Intermediate Language (MSIL) and placed in Assembly Manifest between this compiling time. Both Metadata and MSIL are wrapped together in a Portable Executable (PE) file. Assembly Manifest contains information about itself. This information is called Assembly Manifest, and it includes information about the types, references, members, and all the other data that the runtime requires for execution.

Every assembly you create contains one or more program files and a Manifest. Process Assemblies (EXE) and

Library Assemblies are the two sorts of software files (DLL). There can only be one input point per assembly (DllMain, WinMain, or Main).

Assemblies are two types:

1. **Shared Assembly:** Assemblies that are possible to be used in more than one project are known as a shared assembly. These are usually inducted into the global assembly cache (GAC). Assemblies that are established in the GAC are made available to all the .NET applications on that machine.

2. **Private Assembly:** It is an assembly that is being used by only a single application. Imagine that we have a project now in which we mention to a DLL, so when we develop that particular project, that DLL will be copied to the bin folder of our project. That DLL becomes a private assembly within our project. Usually, the DLLs that are meant for a specific project are private assemblies.

Satellite Assembly and Shared Assembly are the other types of assemblies in .NET.

GAC

GAC stands for Global Assembly Cache, a memory typically used to store the assemblies that are supposed to be used by other different applications.

All computers with CLR installed need to have a GAC as its location can be seen at "C:\Windows\assembly" for

.NET applications with frameworks up to 3.5. For higher frameworks like 4 and 4.5, the GAC can be seen at:

- "C:\Windows\Microsoft.NET\assembly\GAC_MSIL."

The characteristics of assemblies are as follows:

- .exe or .dll files are used to implement assemblies.

We can share assemblies between applications for libraries that specifically select the .NET Framework by placing them in the GAC. You should have strong-name assemblies before you can insert all of them in the GAC.

Assembly files are loaded into memory only when they are required. They aren't loaded if they are not used. This does mean that assemblies can be an efficient way to cope with resources in larger projects.

You can programmatically acquire information about an assembly by using reflection.

You can simply load an assembly to monitor it using the MetadataLoadContext class in .NET Core and the Assembly.ReflectionOnlyLoad or Assembly.ReflectionOnlyLoadFrom methods in .NET Core and .NET Framework

Assembly Manifest

A manifest assembly file is required for every assembly. Similar to a table of contents, the assembly manifest includes

- The assembly's identity (its name and version).

A file table elaborates all the other files that make up the assembly, such as other assemblies you developed that your .exe or .dll file banks on, bitmap files, or Readme files.

An assembly reference list is, in essence, a list of all external dependencies, such as .dlls or other files. Assembly references include references to both global and private objects. Global objects are accessible to all other applications. In .NET Core, global objects are coupled with a particular .NET Core runtime. In .NET Framework, global objects house in the GAC. System.IO.dll is a perfect example of an assembly in the GAC. Private objects must be in a directory level at or below the directory in which your app is installed.

What Are the Benefits of Using Assemblies?

Assemblies are mainly introduced to sort out the problems of versioning, DLL conflicts, and simplifying deployment.

Most end users have experienced versioning or deployment issues when installing a new version or a new application of an existing one. There are many circumstances where you install a new application only to find an existing one stopped working, and the system cannot recover from that. Many developers spent much of their time retaining the registry entries consistency to activate a COM class. All this frustration happens because of versioning issues that occur with component-based applications.

Versioning Problems

Two versioning problems occur with WIN32 applications. The versioning rules are enforced by the OS and are not between the pieces of an application. Backward compatibility between the new part of code and the old one is the current way of versioning, and this is almost impossible to maintain in most applications. Besides that, only a single version of an application is admitted and executed on a computer at any given point in time. The second issue is that there is no way to maintain consistency between components created together and the current present group at run time.

DLL Conflicts

As a result of the above two versioning problems, DLL conflicts do emerge. When installing a new application, an existing one may break because the new one installed a new version of a component or a DLL that is not fully backward compatible enough with the previous one.

The Solution

To sort out the above problems, Microsoft started a sophisticated way in its Windows 2000 platform. Windows 2000 provides you the capacity to place DLL files used by your application in the same directory as your application's exe file to convince use the correct version designed for use. Besides that, Windows 2000 locks files that exist in the System32 directory to prevent their replacement when newer applications are installed, and this contains the DLLs used by existing applications from being replaced and so avert the crashing of existing applications.

The .NET framework established assemblies as an evolution toward the complete solution of versioning problems and DLL conflicts. Assemblies on their core design allow developers to specify version rules between components, offer the infrastructure required to impose these rules, and enable different versions of the part to be run side by side simultaneously.

How Does It Work?

You may be aware that an assembly manifest contains the versioning requirements of the current assembly. The version of the assembly and the versions of the required assemblies and components are included in the manifest. So, when you run on an application, the .NET runtime examines your application's assembly manifest and executes the version of assemblies or components included in the manifest. If you want to get advantages of versioning, you must provide your assembly a firm name.

To use an assembly in an application, you have to attach a reference to it. Once an assembly is referenced, all the accessible types, methods, properties, and other members of its namespaces are accessible to your application as if their code were part of your source file.

CHAPTER 3

Data Types and Operators

IN THIS CHAPTER

- ➤ Basic Data Types
- ➤ Variables
- ➤ Constants
- ➤ Reference Types and Value Types
- ➤ Arrays and Operators

In the previous chapter, we have covered about the building block of C#, The .NET Frameworks, and Assemblies in. NET, and now we will discuss Data Types and Variables. A desktop application, scripted in any programming language, comprises three elements: data, operations on data, and the logic that determines the operations. Therefore, manipulating the data (i.e., holding and operating on it) is at the core of a typical computer program. Variables store the data, and the operations are made by using operators. A data type is a classification of data that tells the compiler or interpreter how the programmer intends to use the data. A data type stands for the type of data that a variable able to store, such as integer, floating, character, etc.

There are three kind of Data Types in C#.

Types	Data Type
Value Data Type	Short, int, char, float, double, etc.
Reference Data Type	String, class, objects, and interface
Pointer Data Type	Pointers

VALUE DATA TYPE

The value data types are integer-based and floating-point based. C# language supports both signed and unsigned literals.

There are two types of value data type in C# language:

1. **Predefined Data Types:** includes values like Integer, Boolean, Float

2. **User-defined Data Types:** consists of Structure and Enumerations

The memory size of data types may vary from 32 or 64 bit operating system.

Let's take a look at the value data types size, given according to 32 bit OS:[1]

<Char	1 byte	-128 to 127
Signed char	1 byte	-128 to 127
Unsigned char	1 byte	0 to 127
Short	2 byte	2 byte
Signed short	2 byte	-32,768 to 32,767
Unsigned short	2 byte	0 to 65,535
Int	4 byte	-2,147,483,648 to -2,147,483,647
Signed int	4 byte	-2,147,483,648 to -2,147,483,647
Unsigned int	4 byte	0 to 4,294,967,295
Long	8 byte	?9,223,372,036,854,775,808 to 9,223,372,036,854,775,807
Signed long	8 byte	?9,223,372,036,854,775,808 to 9,223,372,036,854,775,807
Unsigned long	8 byte	0 - 18,446,744,073,709,551,615
Float	4 byte	$1.5 * 10-45 - 3.4 * 1038$, 7-digit precision
Double	8 byte	$5.0 * 10-324 - 1.7 * 10308$, 15-digit precision
Decimal	16 byte	at least $-7.9 * 10?28 - 7.9 * 1028$, with at least 28-digit precision

REFERENCE DATA TYPE

This particular data types do not include the real data stored in a variable, but they have a certain reference to the variables.

Thus, in case the data is edited by one of the variables, the next variable will immediately return this modification in value.

---

[1] https://www.javatpoint.com/csharp-data-types, Javatpoint

There are two kinds of reference data types in the C# language.

1. **Predefined Types:** such as objects, string.

2. **User-defined Types:** such as classes, interface.

Pointer Data Type

The pointer in the C# language is a variable, and it is also known as a locator or indicator that indicates an address of a value.

Operators

Operators are the basic foundation of any programming language.[2] Thus the functionality of C# language is insufficient without the use of operators. Operators let us perform different types of operations on operands. In C#, operators can be categorized according to their different functionality:

- Arithmetic operators.

- Relational operators.

- Logical operators.

- Bitwise operators.

- Assignment operators.

- Conditional operator

---

[2] C# Operators: Arithmetic, Relational, Assignment And Logical (2019), Software Testing Help

In C#, operators can also be categorized based upon the number of operands:

1. **Unary operator:** Operator that picks one operand to perform the operation.

2. **Binary operator:** Operator that picks two operands to perform the operation.

3. **Ternary operator:** Operator that picks three operands to perform the operation.

We will look into the details of different operators in the last part of this chapter.

BASIC DATA TYPES IN C#

The C# language brings with a set of basic data types. These data types are always used to build values that are applied within an application. Let's dive into the basic data types out there in C#. For every example, we will modify just the main function in our Program. Cs file.

Integer

An Integer data types are always to operate with numbers. And when we say numbers, we specifically mean the whole numbers such as 20, 30, or 40. Additionally, in C# the datatype is marked by the Int32 keyword. Let us look at example of how this data type can be used. In our example, we will expound an Int32 variable called num

```
using System;
using System.Collections.Generic;
using System.Linq;
```

```
using System. Text;
using System.Threading.Tasks;
namespace DemoApplication
{
 class Program
 {
  static void Main(string[] args)
  {
   Int32 num=30;
   Console.Write(num);
   Console.ReadKey();
  }
 }
}
```

- **Code explanation:** The above Int32 data type is set to include an Integer variable called num. The variable is then given a value of 30.

  As for the console, make sure you add function that is used to reflect the number to the console.

Double

A double data type is great to operate with decimals. Similar to the above data type, the numbers should be the whole numbers like 20.21, 30.32, or 40.43. This particular datatype is marked by the keyword "Double." To illustrate with an example:

```
using System;
using System.Collections.Generic;
using System.Linq;
using System.Text;
using System.Threading.Tasks;
```

```
namespace DemoApplication
{
 class Program
 {
  static void Main(string[] args)
  {
   double num=30.33;
   Console.Write(num);
   Console.ReadKey();
  }
 }
}
```

- **Code explanation:** The double data type is set to indicate a double type variable named num. After that the variable is given a value of 30.33.

    As for the console, you are expected to include function used to reflect the number to the console.

Boolean

A Boolean data type is mostly applied when operating with Boolean values of true and false. This datatype is marked by the Boolean keyword. Let's see how this datatype can be used in the following example:

```
using System;
using System.Collections.Generic;
using System.Linq;
using System. Text;
using System.Threading.Tasks;
namespace DemoApplication
{
 class Program
```

```
{
 static void Main(string[] args)
 {
  Boolean status=true;
  Console.Write(status);
  Console.ReadKey();
 }
}
}
```

- **Code explanation:** The Boolean data type specifically includes a Boolean variable called "status." The variable is then given a value of true/false. Finally, do not forget about the console value.

String

A String data type is applied to manage String values. The datatype is marked by the keyword "String." To demonstrate an example of this data type, we shall use a String variable called "message":

```
using System;
using System.Collections.Generic;
using System.Linq;
using System.Text;
using System.Threading.Tasks;
namespace DemoApplication
{
 class program
 {
  static void Main(string[] args)
  {
   String message="Hello";
```

```
    Console.Write(message);
    Console.ReadKey();
   }
  }
}
```

- **Code explanation:** The String data type is used to remark a string variable called message. The variable is then given a value of "Hello."

VARIABLES

A variable is a name denoted to a memory location, and all the operations done on the variable result that memory location. In C#, all the variables must be announced prior their application. It is considered the primary unit of storage withing a program. The value provided in a variable can be modified during program execution.[3]

Types of variables:

- Local variables.

- Instance variables or non-static variables.

- Static variables or class variables.

- Constant variables.

- Read-only variables.

Local Variables

A variable specified within a block, method, or a constructor is referred to as a local variable.

---

[3] C# | Types of Variables (2021), *CatsforCats*

These variables are built when the block is entered, or the function is returned after leaving from the block or when the call exits from the function.

The body of these variables can stay only within the block in which the variable is announced. This means that it is possible to access these variables only within that block.

```
// C# program to demonstrate
// the local variables
using System;
class StudentDetails {
        // Method
    public void StudentAge()
    {
            // local variable age
        int age = 0;
         age = age + 10;
        Console.WriteLine("Student age is
: " + age);
    }
    // Main Method
    public static void Main(String[] args)
    {
        // Creating object
        StudentDetails obj = new
StudentDetails();

        // calling the function
        obj.StudentAge();
    }
}
```

- **Output:** Student age is: 10.

As you can see from the above program, the variable "age" is a local variable that belongs to the function StudentAge(). If you try and use the variable age outside StudentAge() function, the compiler will give away an error:

```
// C# program to demonstrate the error
// due to using the local variable
// outside its scope
using System;
class StudentDetails {
     // Method
    public void StudentAge()
    {
        // local variable age
        int age = 0;
        age = age + 10;
    }
    // Main Method
    public static void Main(String[] args)
    {
        // using local variable age outside
it's scope
        Console.WriteLine("Student age is
: " + age);
    }
}
```

- **Error:** The name "age" does not exist in the current context.

Instance Variables or Non-Static Variables

Instance variables or non-static variables are the ones announced in a class yet kept outside any method, constructor, or block. As instance variables are announced in a class, these variables are built when an object of the class is created and removed when the object is omitted. Also, you can apply access specifiers with these variables. To illustrate with an example:

```
// C# program to illustrate the
// Instance variables
using System;
class Marks {
      // These variables are instance
variables.
    // These variables are in a class and
    // are not inside any function
    int engMarks;
    int mathsMarks;
    int phyMarks;
    // Main Method
    public static void Main(String[]
args)
    {

        // first object
        Marks obj1 = new Marks();
        obj1.engMarks = 90;
        obj1.mathsMarks = 80;
        obj1.phyMarks = 93;

        // second object
        Marks obj2 = new Marks();
        obj2.engMarks = 95;
        obj2.mathsMarks = 70;
        obj2.phyMarks = 90;
```

```
          // displaying marks for first
object
          Console.WriteLine("Marks for first
object:");
          Console.WriteLine(obj1.engMarks);
          Console.WriteLine(obj1.mathsMarks);
          Console.WriteLine(obj1.phyMarks);

          // displaying marks for second
object
          Console.WriteLine("Marks for second
object:");
          Console.WriteLine(obj2.engMarks);
          Console.WriteLine(obj2.mathsMarks);
          Console.WriteLine(obj2.phyMarks);
     }
}
```

- **Output:** Marks for the first object:

    - 90

    - 80

    - 93

    Marks for the second object:

    - 95

    - 70

    - 90

In the above Program the variables, engMarks, maths-Marks, phyMarksare stand for basic instance variables. When you see multiple objects as in the above example, each object should be assigned its own copies of instance variables. It is evident from the above output that each object will have its own copy of the instance variable.

Static Variables or Class Variables

Static variables or class variables are the ones specifically announced with the static modifier. These variables are declared the same way as instance variables, with the only difference is that static variables use the static keyword within a class outside any method constructor or block.

Unlike instance variables, we can only assign one copy of a static variable per class irrespective of how many objects we develop. Moreover, static variables are scripted at the start of program implementation and removed automatically when implementation is over.

In order to access static variables, there is no need to create an object of that class; simply access the variable as:

```
class_name.variable_name;
// C# program to illustrate
// the static variables
using System;
class Emp {
    // static variable salary
    static double salary;
    static String name = "Aks";

    // Main Method
    public static void Main(String[] args)
    {
        // accessing static variable
        // without object
```

```
        Emp.salary = 100000;
        Console.WriteLine(Emp.name + "'s
average salary:"
                                + Emp.salary);
    }
}
```

- **Output:** Aks's average salary: 100000

Initialization of non-static variables is correlated with instance creation and constructor calls, so non-static variables can be initialized through the constructor also. We don't initialize a static variable through the constructor because every time constructor calls, it will override the existing value with a new value.

Difference between Instance Variable and Static Variable

Each object will have its own copy of the instance variable, whereas We can only have one copy of a static variable per class irrespective of how many objects we develop.

Changes made in an instance variable using one object will not be considered in other objects as each object has its own copy of the instance variable. In the case of static, changes will be reflected in other objects as static variables are common to all objects of a class.

We can access instance variables through object references, and Static Variables can be accessed directly using the class name.

We can access instance variables through object references, and Static Variables can be accessed directly using the class name.

In the life cycle of a class, a static variable, i.e., is initialized one and only one time, whereas instance variables are initialized for 0 times if no instance is created and n times if n instances are created.

The Syntax for static and instance variables are:

```
class Example
        {
            static int a; // static
variable
            int b;        // instance
variable
        }
```

Constants Variables

If you see a variable that is announced by using the keyword "const" then it is a constant variable, and it can't be edited once after their declaration, so it should be initialized at the time of declaration only. To show the use of constant variables:[4]

```
// C# program to illustrate the
// constant variable
using System;
class Program {
    // instance variable
    int a = 10;

    // static variable
    static int b = 20;
```

[4] https://msblab.com/programming/csharp/c-different-types-of-variables/, Mslab

```
// constant variable
const float max = 50;

// Main Method
public static void Main()
{

    // creating object
    Program obj = new Program();

    // displaying result
    Console.WriteLine("The value of a
is = " + obj.a);
    Console.WriteLine("The value of b
is = " + Program.b);
    Console.WriteLine("The value of
max is = " + Program.max);
    }
}
```

- The value of a is = 10.

- The value of b is = 20.

- The value of max is = 50.

The behavior of constant variables is similar to the behavior of static variables, i.e., initialized one and only one time in the life cycle of a class and didn't require the instance of the class for accessing or initializing.

The difference between a static and constant variable is that static variables can be modified, whereas constant variables can't be modified once declared.

Below program will show the error because no value is provided at the time of constant variable declaration.

```
// C# program to illustrate the
// constant variables
using System;
class Program {

    // constant variable max
    // but no value is provided
    const float max;

    // Main Method
    public static void Main()
    {

        // creating object
        Program obj = new Program();

        // it will give  error
        Console.WriteLine("The value of b
is = " + Program.b);
    }
}
```

- **Error:** prog.cs(8,17): error CS0145: A const field requires a value to be provided.

Read-Only Variables

In case a variable is marked by using the read-only key-word, then it will be read-only variables, and these variables can't be optimized like constants but after initialization.

It's not necessary to initialize a read-only variable at the time of the declaration, and it can also be done under the constructor. To illustrate the initialization of read-only variable in the constructor:[5]

```
// C# program to illustrate the
// initialization of readonly
// variables in the constructor
using System;
class Cats {
    // instance variable
    int a = 80;

    // static variable
    static int b = 40;

    // Constant variables
    const float max = 50;

    // readonly variables
    readonly int k;

    // constructor
    public Cats()
    {

        // initializing readonly //
variable k
        this.k = 90;
    }
```

5 https://mslab.com/programming/csharp/c-different-types-of-variables/, Mslab

```
    // Main Method
    public static void Main()
    {

        // Creating object
        Cats obj = new Cats();

        Console.WriteLine("The value of a
is = " + obj.a);
        Console.WriteLine("The value of b
is = " + Cats.b);
        Console.WriteLine("The value of
max is = " + Cats.max);
        Console.WriteLine("The value of k
is = " + obj.k);
    }
}
```

- **Output:**
  The value of a is = 80.
  The value of b is = 40.
  The value of max is = 50.
  The value of k is = 90.

CONSTANTS

We have discussed a lot with variables, that can always be changed. The opposite of that is a constant, declared in C# with the keyword const. When declaring a constant, you should assign a value to it immediately, and after that, no alterations can be made to the value of this constant. This is great when you have a value that doesn't change, and you want to make sure that it's not omitted by your code, even by accident.

You will find many constants in the framework itself, e.g., in the Math class, where a constant for pi (3.14) has been defined:

But of course, you should learn how to declare some constants of our own. A constant can be defined in the scope of a method, in the following way:

```
+-
static void Main(string[] args)
{
    const int TheAnswerToLife = 42;
    Console.WriteLine("The answer to life,
the universe and everything: " +
TheAnswerToLife);
}
```

However, most constants are declared on the class level so that they can be accessed (but not changed, of course) from all class methods and even outside of the class, depending on the visibility. A constant will act as a static member of the class, meaning that you can access it without instantiating the class. With that in mind, let's try a complete example where two constants are defined—a private and a public constant:

```
using System;
namespace Constants
{
    class Program
    {
    static void Main(string[] args)
    {
```

```
        Console.WriteLine("The fake answer
to life: " + SomeClass.TheFakeAnswerToLife);
        Console.WriteLine("The real answer
to life: " +
SomeClass.GetAnswer());
    }
    }
    class SomeClass
    {
    private const int TheAnswerToLife = 42;
    public const int TheFakeAnswerToLife =
43;

    public static int GetAnswer()
    {
        return TheAnswerToLife;
    }
    }
}
```

Notice how I define a class (SomeClass) with two constants. The first is private, so it can only be accessed from the class itself, but the other is public. So, in our main program code, I access both constants differently—first directly, since the fake answer is publicly available, and secondly with the help of the GetAnswer() method.

Which Types Can Be Used as a Constant?

Since constants have to be declared immediately and can't be changed later on, the value you assign to a constant has to be a constant expression. The compiler must evaluate the value already at compile time. This means that numbers, Boolean values, and strings can be used just fine for a constant, while, e.g., a DateTime object can't be used as a constant.

Since the compiler needs to know the value immediately, it also means that there are some limitations to what we have to do when setting the value. For instance, these are perfect examples of what you CAN do:

```
const int a = 10;
const float b = a * 2.5f;
const string s1 = "Hello, world!";
const string s2 = s1 + " How are you?";
```

On the other hand, you can't use the result of a method call or a nonconstant class member since these are not constant expressions. Let us discuss some examples of what you can't do:

```
// NOT possible:
const int a = Math.Cos(4) * 2;
// Possible:
const string s1 = "Hello, world!";
// NOT possible:
const string s2 = s1.Substring(0, 6) + "
Universe";
```

The difference lies in what the compiler can be expected to know when it reaches your code, e.g. numbers, strings, and other constants, in contrast to what it has to execute to get the value for.

A Constant Alternative: The Read-Only Field

If you're looking for a slightly less restrictive version of a class constant, you may want to have a look at the read-only keyword. It's not available on the method level. Still, it can be used on the class level to define a field that can only be modified during declaration or the execution of the class's constructor method. So, as soon as the object is available for use, the read-only field will have the same value forever and can't be modified by the user. Let's try it out:

```
class SomeClass
{
    private readonly DateTime rightNow;
    public readonly DateTime later =
DateTime.Now.AddHours(2);
    public SomeClass()
    {
    this.rightNow = DateTime.Now;
    }
}
```

So, we have two read-only fields: The first is private, the second one is public (we usually have properties for that, but bear with me here). The first is declared without a value (we can do that with read-only fields, unlike with constants), while the other one is initialized immediately. You will also notice that we're using the DateTime class as the data type, and we assign a nonconstant value to it. In other words, we do a lot of stuff that we can't do with constants, making read-only fields an excellent alternative to constants.

Notice how we assign a value to the rightNow field in the constructor of the SomeClass class. As already mentioned, this is the last chance to give a value to a read-only field. After that, whether you are in a method inside the defining class or outside, you will get a compile error if you give a value to a read-only field.

REFERENCE TYPE AND VALUE TYPES

Data types in C# have two distinct flavors: value types and reference types. In order to get the difference, it helps to contemplate how space is allocated in C#. Whenever a method is called, the space that has to execute that method is allotted from a data structure called the call stack. The space for a method contains its local variables, including its parameters, but it has exceptions like out or ref parameters.

Value types are two kinds:

1. structures

2. enumerations

Typically, structures contain numeric types such as int, double, and char.

Because value types are stored entirely in variables, whenever a value is allocated to a variable of a value type, the entire value should be written to the variable. For performance reasons, value types, therefore, should be significantly small.

In the case of reference types, the values are not saved directly into the space allotted for the variable. Instead, the variable saves a reference, which is like an address where the value of the variable can definitely be found. When a reference type is developed with a new expression, space for that instance is allocated from a large data structure called the heap (which is unrelated to a heap used to implement a priority queue).

The heap basically stands for a large pool of available memory from which space of multiple sizes may be allocated at any time. It is more complex and less efficient than the stack. When space for a reference type is allotted from the heap, a reference to that space is saved in the variable.

Larger data types are more productively implemented as reference types as an assignment to a variable of a reference type only required to write a reference, not the entire data value.

At the same time, there are three kinds of reference types:

1. classes

2. interfaces

3. delegates

Delegates are used to represent individual methods and are beyond the scope of this course.

Variables of a reference type do not need to refer to any data value. In this case, they store a value of null (variables of a value type cannot store null). Any attempt to access a method, property, or another member of a null or to apply an index to it will result in a NullReferenceException.

The fields of classes or structures are stored depending on whether the field is a value type or a reference type. If it is a value type, the value is directed in the field, regardless of whether that field belongs to an object allocated from the stack or the heap. If it is a reference type, it stores either null or a reference to an object allocated from the heap.

The difference between value types and reference types can be illustrated with the following code example:[6]

```
private int[] DoSomething(int i, int j)
{
    Point a = new Point(i, j);
    Point b = a;
    a.X = i + j;
    int[] c = new int[10];
```

---

[6] https://cis300.cs.ksu.edu/appendix/syntax/reference-value/, Cis300

```
    int[] d = c;
    c[0] = b.X;
    return d;
}
```

Suppose this method is called as follows:

```
int[] values = DoSomething(1, 2);
```

The method contains six local variables: i, j, a, b, c, and d. int is a structure, and hence a value type. Point is a structure (and hence a value type) containing public int properties X and Y, each of which can be read or modified. int[ ], however, is a reference type. Space for all six of these variables is allocated from the stack, and the space for the two points includes space to store two int fields for each. The values 1 and 2 passed for i and j, respectively, are stored directly in these variables.

ARRAYS AND OPERATORS

Arrays could be defined as collections of items, for example, strings. You can apply them to collect items in a single group, and complete various operations on them, like sorting. Moreover, several methods within the framework work on arrays to make it possible to accept a range of items instead of just one. This fact alone makes it important to know a bit about arrays.

Arrays are initiated similar to variables, with a set of [] brackets after the data type, like this:

```
string[] names;
```

You need to instantiate the array to be able to use it, which is done like this:

```
string[] names = new string[2];
```

The number (2) is the size of the array, that is, the number of items we can put in it. Putting items into the array is pretty simple as well:

```
names[0] = "John Smith";
```

The most common way of getting data out of an array is to loop through it and perform some sort of operation with each value. Let's use the array from before, to make a real example:[7]

```
using System;
using System. Collections;
namespace ConsoleApplication1
{
    class Program
    {
    static void Main(string[] args)
    {
        string[] names = new string[2];
        names[0] = "John Doe";
        names[1] = "Jane Doe";
        foreach(string s in names)
        Console.WriteLine(s);
        Console.ReadLine();
    }
    }
}
```

We use the foreach loop, because it's the simplest way, but of course it is possible to use one of the other types of

---

[7] https://a1tutorials.blogspot.com/2014/09/arrays.html, a1tutorials

loop instead. The for loop is good with arrays as well, for instance if you need to count each item, like this:

```
for(int i = 0; i < names.Length; i++)
Console.WriteLine("Item number " + i + ":
" + names[i]);
```

We use the above Length property of the array to see how many times the loop should iterate, and then we use the counter (i) to output where we are in the process, as well as get the item from the array. Just like we used a number, a so called indexer, to put items into the array, we can use it to get a specific item out again.

You could use an array to sort a range of values, and it's very straightforward. The array class holds a bunch of smart methods for working with arrays. This example uses numbers instead of strings, just to try something else, but it could just as easily have been strings. I wish to show you another way of populating an array, which is much easier if you have a small, predefined set of items that you wish to put into your array. Take a look:

```
int[] numbers = new int[5] { 4, 3, 8, 0, 5 };
```

With one line, we have created an array with a size of 5, and filled it with 5 integers. By filling the array like this, you get an extra advantage, since the compiler will check and make sure that you don't insert too many items into the array. Try adding a number more—you will see the compiler notify about the potential error.

The arrays we have used so far have only had one dimension. However, C# arrays can also be multidimensional, sometimes referred to as arrays in arrays. Multidimensional arrays come in two types with C#: Rectangular arrays and jagged arrays. The difference is that with rectangular arrays, all the dimensions have to be the same size, hence the name rectangular. A jagged array can have dimensions of different sizes.

OPERATORS

An operator is a symbol that regulate the compiler to complete specific mathematical or logical manipulations. C# has an extensive set of built-in operators and offers the following type of operators:

- Arithmetic operators
- Relational operators
- Logical operators
- Assignment operators
- Misc operators
- Bitwise operators

Arithmetic Operators

The arithmetic operator lets the program execute general algebraic operations against numeric values.

There are five basic operators available in the C# programming language.

1. **Addition (symbol "+"):** Perform the addition of operands.

2. **Subtraction (symbol "-"):** Performs subtraction of operands.

3. **Division (symbol "/"):** execute division of operands.

4. **Multiplication (symbol "*"):** do multiplication on operands.

5. **Modulus (symbol "%"):** Returns reminder post the division of integer.

Example of this is given below:[8]

```
int a = 10;
int b = 5;
int result;
result = a + b;
result = a - b;
result = a * b;
result = a / b;
result = a % b;
```

- The result of the first operation will be 15, that is, the summation to two integers.

- The result of the second operation will be 5, that is, subtraction of two integers.

- The result of the third operation will be 50, that is, multiplication between two integers.

- The result of the fourth operation will be 2, which is an output of the division of two integers.

- The result of the fifth operation will be 0 as there will be no reminder left when two given integers are divided.

[8] https://www.softwaretestinghelp.com/c-sharp/csharp-operators/, Softwaretestinghelp

You have to remember that the result of the operation will depend upon the data type used to store the result.

So, if the division of two integer values returns a float value and if the result is designated to an integer variable, then the decimal part will be lost because of different data types.

The modulus operator is not like the other operators, it returns the value of the remainder from the division of integers. That is, if we divide 20 by 6, then the division operator will return an answer as 3 (the quotient), and the modulus operator will return two, i.e., the remainder of the division.

Not only have the above five defined operators, but C# also offers two special operators that increase or decrease the value of a variable by 1.

These are:

1. **Increment operator: Denoted by the symbol "++"**

2. **Decrement operator: Denoted by the symbol "- -"**

These operators can be prefixed or suffixed with variables for operation.

Example:

```
int a = 10;
int b = 5;
int increment;
int decrement;
increment = a++;
decrement = b--;
```

In the aforementioned example, the answer for increment will be 11, i.e., the value of a will be increased by 1. While the answer for decrement will be 4, i.e., the value of b will be decreased by 1.

Relational Operators

Any relation between the two operands is approved by using relational operators. Relational operators return Boolean values. If the relation between two operands is successfully validated, then it will return "true," and if the validation fails, then "false" will be returned.

Relational operators are mainly used in decision-making or for defining conditions for loops.

Let's have a look at the Relational Operators offered by C#:[9]

- **Greater than operator: (denoted by ">"):** Validates greater than the relation between operands.

- **Less than operator: (denoted by "<"):** Validates less than the relation between operands.

- **Equals to operator: (denoted by "=="):** Validates the equality of two operands.

- **Greater than or equals to (denoted by ">="):** Validates greater than or equals to the relation between the two operands.

- **Less than or equals to (denoted by "<="):** Validates less than or equals to the relations between the two operands.

- **Not equal: (denoted by "!="):** Validates not an equal relationship between the two operands.

---

[9] https://www.softwaretestinghelp.com/c-sharp/csharp-operators/, softwaretestinghelp

Logical Operators

Logical operators are used for performing logical operations. Logical operators work with Boolean expressions
and return a Boolean value. Logical operators are used
with the conditional operators in loops and decision-making statements.

Logical operators and their usage.

- Logical AND operator
  Symbol: "&&"

  AND operator returns true when both the values are
  true. If any of the value is false then it will return
  false.

  For example, A && B will return true if both A and
  B are true, if any or both of them are false then it will
  return false.

- Logical OR operator
  Symbol: "||"

  Logical NOT operator OR operator returns true if
  any of the condition/operands is true. It will return
  false when both of the operands are false.

  For example, A || B returns true if the value of
  either of A or B is true. It will return false if both A
  and B have false values.
  Symbol: "!"

Assignment Operators

Assignment operators are used for assigning value to a
variable. These are generally used before an arithmetic
operator.

Let's have a look at the Assignment Operators offered by C#:

- **Equals to ("="):** It is one of the simplest assignment operators. It assigns the value of one operand to another. For example, the value of the right side operand to the left side operand.

  - **Example:** a = b

- **Add Equal to the Assignment Operator:** As the name suggests it is a combination of plus "+" and equal to "=". It is written as "+=" and it adds the operand at the right side to the left operand and stores the final value in the left operand.

  - **Example:** a +=b means (a = a + b)

- **Subtract Equal Assignment Operator:** Similar to the add equals, it subtracts the value of the right operand from the left operand and then assigns the value to the left operand.

  - **Example:** a -=b means (a = a-b)

- **Division Equal to the Assignment Operator:** It divides the value of the right operand with the left operand and then stores the result in the left operand.

  - **Example:** a /= b mean (a = a/b)

- **Multiply Equal to the Assignment Operator:** It multiplies the value of the right operand with the left operand and then stores the result in the left operand.

  - **Example:** a *= b mean (a = a*b)

- **Modulus Equals to the Assignment Operator:** It finds the modulus of the left and right operand and stores the value in the left operand.

  - **Example:** a % = b means (a = a%b)

Given below is a program to have more clarity:[10]

```
int a = 10;
int b = 5;
a += b;                 //1
Console.WriteLine(a);
 a -= b;                //2
Console.WriteLine(a);
a /= b;            //3
Console.WriteLine(a);
 a *= b;                //4
Console.WriteLine(a);
a %= b;                 //5
Console.WriteLine(a);
```

- **Output:**
  The first value will return 15, i.e., a = a + b.
  The second operator will return 10, i.e., a = a-b.
  The third operator will return 2, i.e., a = a/b.
  The fourth operator will return 50, i.e., a = a*b.
  The fifth operator will return 0, i.e., a = a%b.

---

[10] https://www.softwaretestinghelp.com/c-sharp/csharp-operators/, softwaretestinghelp

Additional Operators worth-mentioning include the following:

Operator	Description	Example
Sizeof()	Yields the size of a specified variable	Sizeof(a), where a is the integer will return 4
&	Return the address of a variable	&a; returns the actual address of the variable
*	Pointer to a variable	*a:
?:	Conditional Expression	If condition is true? Then value x: Otherwise value Y

To illustrate with an example:[11]

```
/*A C Program for Misc. Operators*/
#include <stdio.h>
int main()
{
int num1 = 4;
short num2;
double num3;
int* ptr;

/* example of sizeof operator */
printf("Line 1 - Size of variable num1 =
%d\n", sizeof(num1) );
printf("Line 2 - Size of variable num2 =
%d\n", sizeof(num2) );
printf("Line 3 - Size of variable num3=
%d\n", sizeof(num3) );
```

---

[11] https://www.softwaretestinghelp.com/c-sharp/csharp-operators/, softwaretestinghelp

```
/* example of & and * operators */
ptr = &num1; /* 'ptr' now contains the
address of 'a'*/
printf("Value of num1 is %d\n", num1);
printf("*ptr is %d.\n", *ptr);

/* example of ternary operator */
num1 = 10;
num2 = (num1 == 1)?  20: 30;
printf( "Value of num2 is %d\n", num2 );
num2 = (num1 == 10)?  20: 30;
printf( "Value of num2 is %d\n", num2 );
return 0;
}
```

- **Output:**
  Value of num1 is 4.
  *ptr is 4.
  Value of num2 is 30.
  Value of num2 is 20.

CHAPTER 4

Exploring User-Defined Types

IN THIS CHAPTER

➤ Classes and Objects

➤ Structures

➤ Enumeration

➤ Namespaces

In this chapter, we will learn how to create custom user types using classes, structures, and enumerations. We will explore what fields, properties, methods, indexers, and constructors are in a class. We will study the access modifiers in C# and learn how to use them to define the visibility of types and members.

A class is a logical collection of similar types of objects. It is one of the most basic types in C#. It is a data structure

DOI: 10.1201/9781003214779-4

that is a combination of methods, functions, and fields. It defines the dynamic instances, i.e., objects that need to be created for the class.

An object in a programming language is almost similar to a real-world object. Object-Oriented Programming is an idea where the programs are designed using sets of classes and objects to simplify program development and maintenance.

CLASSES AND OBJECTS

A class in C# is explained by the keyword class, followed by an identifier (name) of the class and data members and methods in a different code block.

Classes in C# can include the following elements:

- **Fields:** member-variables from a particular type.

- **Properties:** These are particular types of elements that extend the functionality of the fields by giving extra data management when extracting and recording it in the class fields.

- **Methods:** They devise the manipulation of the data.

We will give an example of a class in C#, which includes the listed elements. The class Cat models the real-world object "cat" and has the properties' exact name and color. The given class defines several methods, fields, and properties. So let us see the definition of the class.

```
public class Cat
{
    // Field name
    private string name;
```

```
// Field color
private string color;
public string Name
{
    // Getter of the property "Name."
    get
    {
        return this.name;
    }
    // Setter of the property "Name"
    set
    {
        this.name = value;
    }
}
public string Color
{
    // Getter of the property "Color"
    get
    {
        return this.color;
    }
    // Setter of the property "Color"
    set
    {
        this.color = value;
    }
}

// Default constructor
public Cat()
{
    this.name = "Unnamed";
    this.color = "gray";
}
```

```
    // Constructor with parameters
    public Cat (string name, string color)
    {
        this.name = name;
        this.color = color;
    }

    // Method SayMiau
    public void SayMiau()
    {
        Console.WriteLine("Cat {0} said:
Miauuuuuu!", name);
    }
}
```

The example class Cat explain the properties name and color, which in turn keep their values in the hidden (private) fields name and color. Not only that, two constructors are defined for developing instances of the class Cat, respectively, with and without parameters, and a method of the class SayMiau().

After the example class is defined, we can now move on to use it in the following way:

```
static void Main()
{
    Cat firstCat = new Cat();
    firstCat.Name = "Tony";
    firstCat.SayMiau();

    Cat secondCat = new Cat("Pepy", "red");
    secondCat.SayMiau();
    Console.WriteLine("Cat {0} is {1}.",
        secondCat.Name, secondCat.Color);
}
```

If we run the example, we will get the following output:

- Cat Tony said: Miauuuuuu!

- Cat Pepy said: Miauuuuuu!

- Cat Pepy is Red.

We saw a lucid example for defining and using classes, and in the section "Creating and Using Objects," we are going to explain in detail how to create objects, how to access their properties, and how to call their methods, and this will help us to understand how this example works.

System Classes

Calling the method Console.WriteLine(…) of the class System. The console is an example of the usage of a system class in C#. We can define system classes the classes defined in standard libraries for building applications with C# (or another programming language). They can be used in .NET applications (in particular those written in C#). Such are, for example, the classes String, Math, and Environment.

As we are already may aware that the .NET Framework SDK comes with a set of programming languages (like C# and VB.NET), compilers, and a standard class library that gives thousands of system classes for accomplishing the most common tasks in programming like text processing, console-based input/output, collection classes, networking, parallel execution, database access, data processing, as well as developing web-based, Graphical User Interface (GUI), and mobile applications.

It is essential to know that the implementation of the logic in classes is encapsulated (hidden) inside them. For the programmer, it is vital what they do, not how they do it, and for this reason, a significant part of the classes is not publicly accessible (public). With system classes, the implementation is sometimes not accessible at all to the programmer. Thus, new layers of abstraction are built, which is one of the fundamental principles in OOP.

Creating and Using Objects

Let us focus on creating and using objects in our programs, and it is doing with already well defined classes and mostly with system classes from .NET Framework.

The creation of objects from preliminarily defined classes during program implementation is done by the operator new. The newly created object is often assigned to the variable from type coinciding with the class of the object. We will note that in this assignment, the object is not copied, and only a reference to the newly created object is recorded in the variable (its address in the memory). Here is a simple example of how it works:

```
Cat someCat = new Cat();
```

The variable someCat of type Cat, we appropriate the newly created instance of the class Cat. The variable someCat remains in the stack, and its value (the instance of the class Cat) remains in the managed heap.

Now, we will take up a slightly different variant of the example above in which we set parameters when creating the object:

```
Cat someCat = new Cat("Jack", "brown");
```

In this case, we would like the objects someCat to represent a cat whose name is "Jack" and is brown. We indicate this by using the words "Jack" and "brown," written in the brackets after the name of the class.

When creating an object with the operator new, two things would happen: Memory is set aside for this object, and its data members are initialized. The initialization is performed by a unique method called constructor. In the example above, the initializing parameters are really parameters of the constructor of the class.

As the member variables name and color of the class Cat are of a reference type (of the class String), they are also recorded in the dynamic memory (heap), and in the object itself are kept their references (addresses/pointers).

Releasing the Objects

An essential feature of working with objects in C# is that there is no need to manually tear them down and release the memory taken up by them. This is possible because of the embedded in .NET CLR system for cleaning the memory (garbage collector), which takes care of releasing unused objects instead of us. Objects to which there is no reference in the program at a particular moment instinctively released, and the memory they take up is released. This way, many potential bugs, and problems are controlled. If we would like to release a specific object manually, we have to destroy the reference to it, for example, this way:

```
someCat = null;
```

Access to Fields of an Object

The operator does the access to the fields and properties of a given object.[1] (dot) placed between the names of the object and the name of the field (or the property). The operator is not necessary in case we access field or property of a given class in the body of a method of the same class.

We can either access the fields and the properties to extract data from them or assign new data. In a property, the access is implemented in the same way as in a field—C# gives us this ability. The keywords achieve this get and set in the definition of the property, which performs respectively extraction of the value of the property and assignment of a new value. In the description of the class Cat (given above), the properties are Name and Color.

Access to the Memory and Properties of an Object—Example

We will give an example of using a property of an object and using the already explained above class Cat. We develop an instance myCat of the class Cat and assign "James" to the property Name. After that, we print on the standard output a formatted string with the name of our Cat. You can see an implementation of the example:

```
class CatManipulating
{
    static void Main()
    {
        Cat myCat = new Cat();
```

[1] Svetlin Nakov and Team,(2013),Fundamentals of Computer Programming with C#, *creating and using objects*

```
        myCat.Name = "James";
        Console.WriteLine("The name of my
cat is {0}.",
            myCat.Name);
    }
}
```

Calling Methods of Objects

Calling the methods of a given object is done through the invocation operator () and with the help of the operator. (dot). The operator dot is not obligatory only if the method is called in the body of another method of the same class. Calling a method is performed by its name followed by () or (<parameters>) for the case when we give it some arguments.

Now is the moment to mention that methods of classes have access modifiers private, public, or protected with which the potential to call them could be restricted. For now, it is enough to know that the access modifier public does not introduce any restrictions for calling the method, i.e., makes it publicly available.

Calling Methods of Objects—Example

We will complement the example we already provided as we call the method SayMiau of the class Cat. Here is the result:

```
class CatManipulating
{
    static void Main()
    {
        Cat myCat = new Cat();
```

```
        myCat.Name = "Jack";
        Console.WriteLine("The name of my
cat is {0}.",myCat.Name);
        myCat.SayMiau();
    }
}
```

After executing the program above the following text is going to be printed on the standard output:

- The name of my Cat is Alfred.

- Cat Jack said: Miauuuuuu!

CONSTRUCTORS

The constructor is a special method of the class, which is called automatically when developing an object of this class, and performs initialization of its data (this is its purpose). The constructor has no type of returned value, and its name is not random, and mandatorily coincides with the class name. The constructor can be with or without parameters. A constructor without parameters is also called a parameterless constructor.

Constructor with Parameters

The constructor can take parameters as well as any other method. Each class can have a different count of constructors with one only restriction—the count and type of their parameters have to be different (different signature). When creating an object of this class, one of the constructors is called.

In the presence of several constructors in a class, the question of which of them is called when the object is developed. This problem is sort out in a very intuitive way, as with methods. The compiler automatically chooses the appropriate constructor according to the given bunch of parameters when creating the object. We use the principle of the best match.

Calling Constructors—Example

Let's remind again at the definition of the class Cat and, more specifically, at the two constructors of the class:

```
public class Cat
{
    // Field name
    private string name;
    // Field color
    private string color;
    …
    // Parameterless constructor
    public Cat()
    {
        this.name = "Unnamed";
        this.color = "gray";
    }
    // Constructor with parameters
    public Cat (string name, string color)
    {
        this.name = name;
        this.color = color;
    }
```

We are going to use these constructors to show the usage of constructors with and without parameters. For the class Cat defined that way, we will create its instances by each of the two constructors. One of the objects will be an ordinary undefined cat, and the other is our brown Cat Jack. After that, we will execute the method SayMiau for each of the cats and analyze the result. Source code follows:

```
class CatManipulating
{
    static void Main()
    {

Cat someCat = new Cat();
        someCat.SayMiau();
        Console.WriteLine("The color of
cat {0} is {1}.",
            someCat.Name, someCat.Color);

        Cat someCat = new Cat("Jack",
"brown");
        someCat.SayMiau();
        Console.WriteLine("The color of
cat {0} is {1}.",
            someCat.Name, someCat.Color);
    }
}
```

As a result of the program's execution the following text is printed on the standard output:

- Cat Unnamed said: Miauuuuuu!

- The color of Cat Unnamed is gray.

- Cat Jack said: Miauuuuuu!

- The color of Cat Johnny is brown.

- Static Fields and Methods.

The data members, which we considered until now, implement states of the objects and are directly related to specific classes. In OOP, special categories fields and methods are associated with the data type (class), not the specific instance (object). We call them static members because they are independent of concrete objects. Furthermore, they are used without the need to develop an instance of the class in which they are defined. They can be fields, methods, and constructors. Let's consider shortly static members in C#.

A static field or method in a given class is defined with the keyword static, placed before the type of the field or the type of returned value of the method. When defining a static constructor, the word static is placed before the name of the constructor.

When to Use Static Fields and Methods

To find the answers to this question, we must understand the difference between static and non-static members. We are going to consider into detail what it is.

We have already explained the main difference between the two types of members. Let's paraphrase the class as a category of objects and the object as a representative of this category. Then the static members reflect the state and the behavior of the category itself, and the non-static members represent the state and the behavior of the separate representatives of that particular category.

Now, we will heed special attention to the initialization of static and non-static fields. We are already aware that non-static fields are initialized with the call to the class's constructor when creating an instance of it—either inside the constructor's body or outside. However, the initialization of static fields cannot be performed when the object of the class is created because they can be used without a created instance of the class.

Static Fields and Methods—Example

The example, which we intend to give, solves the following simple problem: We need a method that returns a value greater with one than the value returned at the previous call of the method. We choose the first returned value to be 0. Of course, this method produces the sequence of natural numbers. Similar functionality is explicitly used in practice, for example, for uniform numbering of objects. Now, we will see how this could be implemented with the means of OOP.

Let's imagine that the method is called NextValue() and is defined in a class called Sequence. The class has a field currentValue from type int, which includes the last returned value by the method. We want the following two actions to be performed consecutively in the method body: the value of the field to be increased and its new value to be returned as a result. Obviously, the returned by the method value does not depend on the concrete instance of the class Sequence. For this reason, the method and the field are static. You can now see the described implementation of the class:

```
public class Sequence
{
    // Static field, holding the current
sequence value
    private static int currentValue = 0;
    // Intentionally deny instantiation of
this class
    private Sequence()
```

```
    {
    }
    // Static method for taking the next
sequence value
    public static int NextValue()
    {
        currentValue++;
        return currentValue;
    }
}
```

STRUCTURES

A Structure is a collection of different variables with random variables like Int, Float Char. The C# Language also has a data type that includes all the other data types of int, float, and character. The Main user defines data type as Structure, which provides us the facility to make a data type that holds either the int value or float value of character values.

Structure is the user-defined data type that is used for creating a single variable which makes it possible to declare a value either a int, float, or character A user. Structure is like a container which holds all the other variables with their different values and their different length.

Always remember that the member of the Structure is accessed with the help of the (dot). operator or if we want to access a variable of the structure then we must use the. (dot) operator. For declaring the structure, we can use this syntax:

```
struct sta
{
  char name[10],lastname[10];
  int age;
  float height;
}
```

The structure is also user defined data type, but the main difference between the arrays and Structure is that all the components of an array are of the same type. While in structure, all the components are of different data type.

Structs with Methods

A C# Struct can also hold either static or non-static. But static methods can access only other static members, and they can't be called by using an object of the structure. They can be included only by using the struct name. To illustrate with an example:[2]

```
/*Structs with Methods/Function*/
using System;
struct str
{
  int a,b;
  public void get()
  {
    Console.WriteLIne("Enter a No.");
    a = Int32.Parse(Console.ReadLine());
    b = Int32.Parse(Console.ReadLine());
  }
  public void show()
  {
    int c = a + b;
    Console.WriteLine("Sum = " + c);
  }
}
```

---

[2] https://programming-incsharp.blogspot.com/2014/04/structures-and-enu-merations.html, Blogspot

```
class ABC
{
  public static void Main()
  {
    str obj = new str();
    obj.get();
    obj.show();
  }
}
```

Structs and Constructors

A C# struct can announce constructor, but they must have certain parameters. A default constructor (constructor without any parameters) can be used to initialize the struct fields to their default values. The parameterized constructors inside a struct can also be overload.

```
/*Structs and Constructors */
using System;
struct str
{
  int a,b;
  public str()
//Error, we can't use default structure of
constructor
    a = 100;
    b = 200;
  }
  public void show()
  {
    int c = a + b;
    Console.WriteLine("Sum="+c);
  }
}
```

```
class student
{
  public static void Main()
  {
    str obj = new str();
    obj.show();
  }
}
```

Nested Structs

We can declare nested structures, as default structs are placed inside other structs. The following code snippet explains this:

```
/* Nested Structure */
using System;
struct student
{
  public String name, last;
}
struct Marks      //Nested Structure
{
  public student s;
  public int math, sci;
}

class nest
{
  public static void Main()
  {
    Marks m;
    m.s.name = "Pardeep";
    m.s.last = "Kumar";
```

```
    m.math = 75;
    m.sci = 70;

    Console.WriteLine("Name = "+m.s.name);
    Console.WriteLine("Last Name =
"+m.s.last);
    Console.WriteLine("Math Marks = "+m.
math);
    Console.WriteLine("Science = "+m.sci);
  }
}
```

It is effortless to use a structure in C#. The following programming example will show you how to create and use a
structure in C# programming:

```
using System;
using System.Collections.Generic;
using System.Linq;
using System.Text;

namespace Structure_Statements
{
    class Program
    {
        // creating three different
variables in a single structure
        struct book
        {
            public string book name;
            public int price;
            public string category;
        }
```

```csharp
static void Main(string[] args)
{
    //Creating two book type
variable
    book language, database;

    // Storing value in language
variable
    Console.Write("Enter book
name:\t");
    language.bookname = Console.
ReadLine();
    Console.Write("Enter book
price:\t");
    language.price = Convert.
ToInt32(Console.ReadLine());
    Console.Write("Enter book
category:\t");
    language.category = Console.
ReadLine();

    //Storing value in database
variable
    Console.Write("\n\nEnter book
name:\t");
    database.bookname = Console.
ReadLine();
    Console.Write("Enter book
price:\t");
    database.price = Convert.
ToInt32(Console.ReadLine());
    Console.Write("Enter book
category:\t");
```

```
            database.category = Console.
ReadLine();

            //Displaying value of language
variable

Console.Write("\n\n===================");
            Console.Write("\n\t\
tLanguage\n");

Console.Write("===================\n\n");
            Console.Write("Book
Name:\t{0}", language.bookname);
            Console.Write("\nBook
Price:\t{0}", language.price);
            Console.Write("\nBook
Category:\t{0}", language.category);

Console.Write("\n\n==================\n");

Console.Write("\t\tDatabase\n");

Console.Write("===================\n\n");
            Console.Write("Book
Name:\t{0}", database.bookname);
            Console.Write("\nBook
Price:\t{0}", database.price);
            Console.Write("\nBook
Category:\t{0}", database.category);

            Console.ReadLine();
        }
    }
}
```

- **Output:**

Enter book name:	C Sharp.
Enter book price:	34.
Enter book category:	Object-Oriented Programming.
Enter book name:	SQL Server.
Enter book price:	23.
Enter book category:	Database Programming.

- **Language:**

Enter book name:	C Sharp.
Enter book price:	34.
Enter book category:	Object-Oriented Programming.

- **Database:**

Enter book name:	SQL Server.
Enter book price:	23.
Enter book category:	Database Programming.

In the above example, we have just created a structure named book that includes three variables as bookname, price, category. These variables can be accessed by creating the object of book structure.

ENUMERATION

Enumeration (or enum) is another value data type in C# that is mainly applied to give the names or string values to integral constants, making the code easy to read and operate with. The main objective of enum is to define our data types (Enumerated Data Types). Enumeration is declared using enum keyword directly inside a namespace, class, or structure.

Syntax:

```
enum Enum_variable
{
      string_1...;
      string_2...;
 .
 .
 .
}
```

In the above syntax, Enum_variable is the name of the enumerator, and string_1 is added with value 0, string_2 is attached value 1, and so on. Since the first member of an enum has the value 0, the value of each successive enum member will be increased by 1. Yet, it is possible to change this default value.

Now, let's consider the below code for the enum. At first, enum with name month is created, and its data members are the name of months like jan, feb, mar, apr, may. With that we print the default integer values of these enums. An explicit cast is required to convert from enum type to an integral type:[3]

```
// C# program to illustrate the enums
// with their default values
using System;
namespace ConsoleApplication1 {

// making an enumerator 'month'
enum month
```

---

[3] https://www.geeksforgeeks.org/c-sharp-tutorial/, geeksforgeeks

```
{

    // following are the data members
    jan,
    feb,
    mar,
    apr,
    may
}
class Program {

    // Main Method
    static void Main(string[] args)
    {

        // getting the integer values of
data members..
        Console.WriteLine("The value of
jan in month " +
                            "enum is " +
(int)month.jan);
        Console.WriteLine("The value of
feb in month " +
                            "enum is " +
(int)month.feb);
        Console.WriteLine("The value of
mar in month " +
                            "enum is " +
(int)month.mar);
        Console.WriteLine("The value of
apr in month " +
                            "enum is " +
(int)month.apr);
        Console.WriteLine("The value of
may in month " +
```

```
                                    "enum is " +
(int)month.may);
    }
}
}
```

- **Output:**
  The value of jan in month enum is 0.
  The value of feb in month enum is 1.
  The value of mar in month enum is 2.
  The value of apr in month enum is 3.
  The value of may in month enum is 4.

As discussed above, that the default value of the first enum member is set to 0, and it increases by 1 for the further data members of enum. However, the user can also change these default value:

```
enum days {
    day1 = 1,
    day2 = day1 + 1,
    day3 = day1 + 2
.
.
}
```

In the above example, day1 is assigned value '1' by the user, day2 will be assigned value '2' and similar is the case with day3 member. So you have to just change the value of the first data member of enum, further data members of enums will increase by 1 than the previous one automatically.

if the data member of enum member has not been initialized, then its value is set according to rules stated below:

- If it is the first member, then its value is set to 0 otherwise.

- It set out the value which is obtained by adding 1 to the previous value of enum data member.

To demonstrate with an example:

```
enum random {
A,
B,
C = 6;
D
}
```

Here, A is set to 0 by default, B will be incremented to 1. However, as C is initialized with 6 so the value of D will be 7.

To demonstrate the initialization of enum data member with user define values and some particular case of initialization:[4]

```
// C# program to illustrate the enum
// data member Initialisation
using System;
namespace ConsoleApplication3 {
// enum declaration
enum days {
        // enum data members
```

---

[4] https://www.geeksforgeeks.org/c-sharp-tutorial/, geeksforgeeks

```
    Monday,
    Tuesday,
    Wednesday,
    Thursday,
    Friday,
    Saturday,
    Sunday
}
// enum declaration
enum color {
    // enum data members
    Red,
    Yellow,
    Blue,
        // assigning value yellow(1) + 5
    Green = Yellow + 5,
    Brown,
    // assigning value yellow(1) + 5
    Green = Yellow + 5,
    Brown,
        // assigning value Green(6) + 3
    Black = Green + 3
}
class Program {
    // Main Method
    static void Main(string[] args)
    {
        Console.WriteLine("Demonstrating
the difference "+
                    "between Special
Initialisation" +
                "cases and non-
initialisation cases\n\n");
        // first of all non-initialized enum
        // 'days' will be displayed
```

```
        // as mentioned already, the first
        // member is initialized to 0
        // hence the output will numbers
        // from 0 1 2 3 4 5 6

        Console.WriteLine("Value of Monday
is " +
                          (int)days.monday);
        Console.WriteLine("Value of Tuesday
is " +
                          (int)days.tuesday);
        Console.WriteLine("Value of
Wednesday is " +

(int)days.wednesday);
        Console.WriteLine("Value of
Thursday is " +
Console.WriteLine("Value of Friday is " +
                          (int)days.friday);
        Console.WriteLine("Value of
Saturday is " +

(int)days.saturday);
        Console.WriteLine("Value of Sunday
is " +

(int)days.sunday);
        // Now the use of special
initialisation
        // cases is demostrated as expected
Red
        // will be assigned 0 value
similarly
        // yellow will be 1 and blue will
be 2
```

```
        // however, green will be assigned
the
        // value 1+5=6 similarly is the case
        // with brown and black
        Console.WriteLine("\n\nColor Enum");
        Console.WriteLine("Value of Red
Color is " +
(int)color.Red);
        Console.WriteLine("Value of Yellow
Color is " +
                        (int)color.Yellow);
        Console.WriteLine("Value of Blue
Color is " +
                        (int)color.Blue);
        Console.WriteLine("Value of Green
Color is " +
                        (int)color.Green);
        Console.WriteLine("Value of Brown
Color is " +
                        (int)color.Brown);
        Console.WriteLine("Value of Black
Color is " +
                        (int)color.Black);
    }
}
```

- **Output:**
  Value of Monday is 0.
  Value of Tuesday is 1.
  Value of Wednesday is 2.
  Value of Thursday is 3.
  Value of Friday is 4.
  Value of Saturday is 5.
  Value of Sunday is 6.

- **Color Enum:**
  Value of Red Color is 0.
  Value of Yellow Color is 1.
  Value of Blue Color is 2.
  Value of Green Color is 6.
  Value of Brown Color is 7.
  Value of Black Color is 9.

NAMESPACES

Namespaces are used to organize the classes.[5] They are great to manage the scope of methods and classes. To put it simply, you can say that it provides a way to keep one set of names (like class names) different from other sets of names. The most important advantage of using namespace is that the class names declared in one namespace will not clash with the same class names displayed in another namespace. It is also referred to as a named group of classes having common features. The items of a namespace can be namespaces, interfaces, structures, and delegates.

In order to define a namespace in C#, we will use the namespace keyword followed by the name of the namespace and curly braces containing the body of the namespace as follows:

```
namespace name_of_namespace {
// Namespace (Nested Namespaces)
// Classes
// Interfaces
// Structures
// Delegates
}
```

---

[5] https://www.geeksforgeeks.org/c-sharp-namespaces/, geeksforgeeks

For example

```
// defining the namespace name1
namespace name1
{
    // C1 is the class in the namespace
name1
    class C1
    {
        // class code
    }
}
```

Please keep in mind that the members of a namespace are accessed by using dot(.) operator. Its respective namespace fully knows a class in C#:

```
[namespace_name] . [member_name]
```

At the same time, remember that two classes with the same name can be created inside two different namespaces in a single program. Inside a namespace, no two classes can have the same name.

In C#, the full name of the class starts from its namespace name followed by dot(.) operator and the class name, which is termed as the fully qualified name of the class. For example:[6]

```
// C# program to illustrate the
// use of namespaces
// namespace declaration
```

---

[6] https://www.geeksforgeeks.org/c-sharp-namespaces/, geeksforgeeks

```
namespace first {
          // name_1 namespace members
    // i.e. class
    class Newsco_1
    {

        // function of class Newsco_1
        public static void display()
        {
            // Here System is the namespace
            // under which Console class
is defined
            // You can avoid writing System
with
            // the help of "using" keyword
discussed
            // later in this article

System.Console.WriteLine("Hello Newsco!");
          }
    }

    /* Removing comment will give the error
       because no two classes can have the
       same name under a single namespace
    class Newsco_1
    {

    }
*/

} // ending of first namespace
```

```
// Class declaration
class Newsco_2
{

    // Main Method
    public static void Main(String []args)
    {
       // calling the display method of
        // class Newsco_1 by using two dot
        // operator as one is use to access
        // the class of first namespace
and
        // another is use to access the
        // static method of class Newsco_1.
        // Termed as fully qualified name
        first.Newsco_1.display();

    }
}
```

The output would then be the following:

- Hello Newsco!

It is not actually practical to call the function or class (or any other members of a namespace) every time by using its fully qualified name. In the above example, System.Console. WriteLine("Hello Newsco!"); and first.Newsco_1.display(); are the fully qualified name. So C# uses a keyword "using" which helps the user to avoid writing fully qualified names every other time. The user has to add the namespace name at the starting of the program, and then he can easily omit using fully qualified names. To demonstrate:[7]

```
// predefined namespace name
using System;
// user-defined namespace name
using name1
// namespace having subnamespace
using System.Collections.Generic;
```

Program:

```
// C# program to illustrate the
// use of using keyword
// predefined namespace
using System;
// user-defined namespace
using first;
  // namespace declaration
namespace first {
    // name_1 namespace members
    // i.e. class
    class Newsco_1
    {
                 // function of class
Geeks_1
        public static void display()
        {
            // No need to write fully
qualified name
```

[7] https://www.geeksforgeeks.org/c-sharp-namespaces/, geeksforgeeks

```
            // as we have used "using
System"
            Console.WriteLine("Hello
Newsco!");
                    }
    }
      } // ending of first namespace
// Class declaration
class Newsco_2
{
        // Main Method
    public static void Main(String []args)
    {
        // calling the display method of
        // class Newsco_1 by using only
one
        // dot operator as display is the
        // static method of class Newsco_1
        Newsco_1.display();

    }
}
```

The final output is:

- Hello Newsco!

Nested Namespaces

As an alternative, you can define a namespace into another namespace which is referred to as the nested namespace. In order to access the members of the nested namespace, user has to use the dot(.) operator.

For instance, Generic is the nested namespace in the collections namespace as System.Collections.Generic and has the following syntax:[8]

```
namespace name_of_namespace_1
{
    // Member declarations & definitions
    namespace name_of_namespace_2
    {
        // Member declarations & definitions
.
.
    }
}
```

Program:

```
// C# program to illustrate use of
// nested namespace
using System;
// You can also use
// using Main_name.Nest_name;
// to avoid the use of fully
// qualified name
  // main namespace
namespace Main_name
{
    // nested namespace
    namespace Nest_name
    {
            // class within nested
namespace
```

[8] https://www.geeksforgeeks.org/c-sharp-namespaces/, geeksforgeeks

```
class Newsco_1
  {
        // Constructor of nested
      // namespace class Geeks_1
      public Newsco_1() {
            Console.
WriteLine("Nested Namespace Constructor");
        }
    }
  }
}

// Driver Class
class Driver
{
        // Main Method
    public static void Main(string[] args)
    {
        // accessing the Nested Namespace
by
        // using fully qualified name
        // "new" is used as Geeks_1()
        // is the Constructor
        new Main_name.Nest_name.Newsco_1();
    }
}
```

The final output would be

- Nested Namespace Constructor.

CHAPTER 5

Object-Oriented Programming in C#

IN THIS CHAPTER

➢ What is OOP

➢ Implementation of OOP

➢ Encapsulation and Inheritance

We have explored user-defined types in the last chapter and now will discuss Object-oriented programming (OOP) in C#. It is a kind of programming structure where programs are arranged around objects as an alternative to action and logic. This is a design that uses a different set of programming languages, such as C#. Understanding OOP concepts can help decide how we should design an application and what language to use.

DOI: 10.1201/9781003214779-5

Everything in OOP is put together as self-sustainable "objects." An object is a combination of functions, variables, and data that performs a set of related activities. When the object performs those activities, it defines the object's behavior. furthermore, an object is an instance of a class.

OOP provides several advantages over the other programming models like:

- The precise and clear modular approach for programs offers easy understanding and maintenance.

- Classes and objects built in the project can be used across the project.

- The modular approach lets different modules exist independently, thereby allowing several other developers to work on different modules together OOP systems can be easily upgraded from small to large systems.

- Multiple instances of objects coexist without any kind of interference.

- It can be possible to map the objects in the problem domain to those in the program.

- By using inheritance, we can definitely eliminate redundant code and extend the use of existing classes.

- Message passing techniques are used for communication between objects which would, in essence, makes the interface descriptions with external systems much more uncomplicated.

- The data-centered design approach help us to capture more details of the model in an implementable form.

- It is effortless to partition the work into a project based on objects.

- The principle of data hiding allow the programmer build secure programs that the code cannot invade in other parts of the program.

WHAT IS OOP

As we discussed above, OOP is a programming model that run on a principle that spin around objects rather than action or logic. It enables the users to create objects based on the requirement and then create methods to operate upon those objects.

Working on these objects to get the desired result is ultimately the goal of OOP.

Basic Principles Concept in C# Programming

- Abstraction.
- Polymorphism.
- Encapsulation.
- Inheritance.

The abstraction gives you focus on what the exact object does instead of how it does and is the process of hiding the working style of an object and showing the information of an object understandably. Polymorphism is the process of using an operator or run in different ways for different data inputs. The encapsulation conceals the implementation details of a class from other objects. The inheritance is a way to form new classes using classes that have already been explained.

Structure of OOP

The building blocks or structure of OOP include the following:

- **Classes:** are user-defined data types that work as the design for individual attributes, methods, and objects.

- **Objects:** are examples of a class developed with precisely defined data. Objects can correspond to real-world objects or abstract entities. When class is defined firstly, the description is the only object that is defined.

- **Attributes:** are specifically marked in the class template and represent the state of an object. Objects normally have data located in the attributes section. And class attributes belong to the class itself.

- **Methods:** are functions that are set inside a class that elaborate the nature of an object. Each method included in class definitions starts with reference to an instance object. Moreover, the subroutines attached to object are referred to as instance methods. Programmers typically apply methods to preserve functionality encapsulated inside one object at a time.

In this, Class and objects are the two main aspects of OOP.

Class

A class is an assembly of objects and represents a description of objects that share the same attributes and actions. It is used to narrate all of the characteristics and behavior of a type of Object.

Once instantiated, an object is generated that has all of the properties, methods, and other behavior defined within the Class.

A class should not be added with an object. The Class is the abstract concept for an object that is created at design time by the programmer. The objects based upon the Class are the concrete instances of the Class that occurs at runtime. For example, the Car class will define that all cars have a make, model, and color. The syntax and declaration example of Class:

```
namespace ClassTest
{
    public class Vehicle
    {
        //your code goes here..
    }
}
```

Instantiating the Class

```
static void Main(string[] args)
{
    Vehicle car = new Vehicle();
    Console.WriteLine(car.ToString());  //
Outputs "ClassTest.Vehicle"
}
```

Objects

Objects are fundamental building blocks of a C# OOP program. An object is a combination of methods and data. The data and the methods are called members of an object. In an OOP program, we develop objects. These objects communicate together through methods. Each Object can send messages, receive messages, and process data.

For creating an object, there are two steps. First, we define a class. A class is actually a template for an object. It is a design that elaborates the state and behavior that the objects of the class all share. A class can be used to create as many objects. Objects made at runtime from a class are called instances of that particular Class.

For example, a "Car" usually has common elements such as Car color, engine, mileage, etc. In OOP terminology, these would be called a Class Properties or Attributes of a Bike object. Here is an example of an Object:

```
public class Car
{
        //This is the class that include
all properties and behavior of an object

        //here are some properties of class
Car
        public string color;
        public string engine;
        public int mileage;
        //here is some behavior of class
Car
        public string GetColor()
```

```
{
        return "red";
}
public int GetMileage()
{
        return 24;
}
}
```

Now, to access Car class, we need to create the object of the Car class and then access its Methods and objects:

```
//It is also considered as an "Instance of
a Car Class"
Car objCar = new Car ();
//Accessing Car class methods
objCar.GetColor();
objCar.GetMileage();
```

Method

Methods are a kind of function defined interior the body of a class. They are used to carry out operations with the attributes of your objects. Methods bring modularity to your programs.

Methods are important in the encapsulation concept of the OOP paradigm as it is clearly explained through an example that we might have a Connect() method in your AccessDatabase class. We need not be aware of how precisely the method Connect() attach to the database. We are only aware that it is used to connect to a database. This is crucial in dividing responsibilities in programming, particularly in large applications.

Objects group state and behavior, and methods represent the behavioral part of the objects:

```
using System;
public class Circle
{
    private int radius;
    public void SetRadius(int radius)
    {
        this.radius = radius;
    }
    public double Area()
    {
        return this.radius * this.radius *
Math.PI;
    }
}
public class Methods
{
    static void Main()
    {
        Circle c = new Circle();
c.SetRadius(5);
        Console.WriteLine(c.Area());
    }
}
```

We have a Circle class in the code example. We define two methods.

1. **private int radius:** We have one member field. It is the radius of the circle. The private keyword is an access specifier. It explains that the variable is restricted to the outside world. If we want to modify this variable

from the outside, we should use the publicly available SetRadius() method. This way, we protect our data.

2. **public void SetRadius(int radius)**

```
{
    this.radius = radius;
}
```

This is the SetRadius() method. This variable is a particular variable which we use to access the member fields from methods. This.radius is an instance variable, while the radius is a local variable, it is valid only inside the SetRadius() method:

```
Circle c = new Circle();
c.SetRadius(5);
```

We make an instance of the Circle class and fix its radius by calling the SetRadius() method on the Object of the circle. We have to use the dot operator to call the method here:

```
public double Area()
{
    return this.radius * this.radius *
Math.PI;
}
```

The Area() method returns the area of a circle.

Encapsulation

Encapsulation is the process of enclosing or keeping one or more items within a single physical or logical package. In OOP methodology, it stops access to implementation details.

Encapsulation is achieved by utilizing access specifiers. An access specifier determines the scope and visibility of a class member. Available access specifiers are public, protected, private, and internal.

How to Achieve Encapsulation   We can reach into encapsulation by using a private access modifier, as shown in the below example method.

```
private string GetEngineMakeFormula()
{
        private string formula = "a*b";
        return formula;
}
```

Example—[Encapsulation]

```
public class Car
{
        public int mileage = 65;
        public string color = "Black";
        private string formula = "a*b";

        //Its public - so accessible outside
class
        public int GetMileage()
        {
                return mileage;
        }
        //Its public - so accessible outside
Class
        public string GetColor()
        {
```

```
                return color;
        }
//Its private - so not accessible outside
class
        private string GetEngineMakeFormula()
        {
                return formula;
        }
}
```

public class Program

```
{
        public static void Main(string[]
args)
        {
                Car objCar = new Car();
                Console.WriteLine("Car
mileage is : " + objCar.GetMileage()); //
accessible outside "Car"
                Console.WriteLine("Car color
is : " + objCar.GetColor()); //accessible
outside "Car"
                //we can't call this method
as it is inaccessible outside "Car"

//objBike.GetEngineMakeFormula(); //
commented because we can't access it
                Console.Read();
        }
}
```

- Car mileage is: 65.

- Car color is: Black

Abstract Classes

In C#, abstraction is achieved with the help of Abstract classes. An abstract class is declared with the help of an abstract keyword.

In C#, you are not permit to create objects of the abstract class. Or in other words, you cannot use the abstract Class directly with the new operator.

Class that includes the abstract keyword with some of its methods(not all abstract methods) is known as an Abstract Base Class. While class that includes the abstract keyword with all of its methods is known as pure Abstract Base Class.

You are not allowed to declare the abstract methods outside the abstract Class. You are not allowed to declare abstract Class as Sealed Class.

For example, we continue with "Car" as an example, and we have no access to the piston directly and use the start button to run the piston. Just imagine if a Car manufacturer allows direct access to the piston, it would be very difficult to control actions on the piston. That's the reason why a Car provider separates its internal implementation from its external interface

```
public class Car
{
        public int mileage = 24;
        public string color = "Black";
        private string formula = "a*b";

        //Its public - so accessible outside
class
```

```csharp
        public int GetMileage()
        {
                return mileage;
        }

        //Its public - so accessible outside
Class
        public string GetColor()
        {
                return color;
        }
//Its private - so not accessible outside
class
        private string
GetEngineMakeFormula()
        {
                return formula;
        }

        //Its public - so accessible outside
Class
        public string DisplayMakeFormula()
        {

//"GetEngineMakeFormula()" is private but
accessible and limited to this class only
                return GetEngineMakeFormula();
        }
}

public class Program
{
```

```
        public static void Main(string[]
args)
        {
                Car objCar = new Car();
                Console.WriteLine("Car
mileage is : " + objCar.GetMileage()); //
accessible outside "Car"

Console.WriteLine("Car color is : " +
objCar.GetColor()); //accessible outside
"Car"
                //we can't call this method
as it is inaccessible outside "Car"
                //objCar.
GetEngineMakeFormula(); //commented because
we can't access it
                Console.WriteLine("Car color
is : " + objCar.DisplayMakeFormula()); //
accessible outside
                Console.Read();
        }
}
```

As you can see from the above code that necessary methods and properties are exposed using public access modifier, and unnecessary methods and properties are hidden using private access modifier. This way, we can implement abstraction, or we can achieve abstraction in our code or web application.

Inheritance
The inheritance is a way to make new classes using classes that have already been defined. The newly formed classes

are called derived classes; the classes that we derive from are called base classes. Important advantages of inheritance are code reuse and reduction of complexity of a program. The derived classes (descendants) override or extend the functionality of the base classes (ancestors). To illustrate with an example:

```
using System;
public class Being
{
    public Being()
    {
        Console.WriteLine("Being is
çreated");
    }
}

public class Human: Being
{
    public Human()
    {
        Console.WriteLine("Human is
created");
    }
}

public class Inheritance
{
static void Main()
    {
        new Human();
    }
}
```

In this program, we have two classes: a base Being class and a derived Human class. The derived class inherits from the base class:

- public class Human: Being

In C#, we use the colon (:) operator to create inheritance relations:

- new Human();

We instantiate the derived Human Class.
The output of the above Inheritance code will be:

- Being is created
- Human is created

We can see that both constructors were called. First, the constructor of the base class is called, then the constructor of the derived Class.

Polymorphism
Polymorphism is could be described as applying an operator or function in various ways for different data inputs.

In practical terms, polymorphism means that if class B inherits from class A, it does not have to inherit everything about class A; meaning it can do some of the things that class A does differently.

Polymorphism also stands for the ability to redefine methods for derived classes. There are two types of polymorphism in C#: compile-time polymorphism and runtime polymorphism.

Compile-time polymorphism is achieved by method overloading and operator overloading in C#. It is also known as static binding or early binding. Let's take a look at the example of Compile time polymorphism:

```
public class clsCalculation
{
        public int Add(int a, int b)
        {
            return a + b;
        }
        public double Add(int z, int x,
int c)
        {
            return z + x + c;
        }
}
```

In the above code, we have a class "clsCalculation" having two functions with the same name, "Add," but having different input parameters.

The first function is with two parameters, and the second function having three parameters. So this type of polymorphism is also known as method overloading.

It is a compile-time polymorphism because the compiler already knows what type of Object it is linking to, what are methods it is going to call it. So linking a method during a compile-time is also called Early binding.

Runtime polymorphism is achieved by method overriding, which is also known as dynamic binding or late binding. Example of the runtime polymorphism would be:[1]

```csharp
using System;
public abstract class Shape
{
    protected int x;
    protected int y;
    public abstract int Area();
}
public class Rectangle : Shape
{
    public Rectangle(int x, int y)
    {
        this.x = x;
        this.y = y;
    }
    public override int Area()
    {
}
public class Square: Shape
{
    public Square(int x)
    {
        this.x = x;
    }
    public override int Area()
    {
        return this.x * this.x;
    }
}
public class Polymorphism
```

---

[1] https://zetcode.com/lang/csharp/oopii/, Zetcode

```
{
    static void Main()
    {
Shape[] shapes = { new Square(5),
            new Rectangle(9, 4), new
Square(12) };
        foreach (Shape shape in shapes)
        {
            Console.WriteLine(shape.
Area());
        }
    }
}
```

In the above program, we have an abstract Shape class. This Class morphs into two descendant classes: Rectangle and Square. Both offer their own implementation of the Area() method:

```
public override int Area()
{
    return this.x * this.y;
}
...
public override int Area()
{
    return this.x * this.x;
}
```

The Rectangle and the Square classes have their implementations of the Area() method.

```
Shape[] shapes = { new Square(5),
    new Rectangle(9, 4), new Square(12) };
```

We create an array of three Shapes.

```
foreach (Shape shape in shapes)
{
    Console.WriteLine(shape.Area());
}
```

You will be expected to go through each shape and call the Area() method on it. The compiler returns the most suitable method for each shape. This defines the essence of polymorphism.

IMPLEMENTATION OF OOP

The main idea behind OOP is to have in a single unit both data and the methods that manage the data; such units are called an object. All OOP languages offer mechanisms that help you implement the object-oriented model—encapsulation, inheritance, polymorphism, and reusability.[2]

Encapsulation

Encapsulation puts together code and the data it regulates keeps them both safe. Encapsulation is a protective tool that prevent code and data from being hacked by other code located outside the container.

Inheritance

Inheritance is the process by which one object receives the properties of another object. Inheritance is most useful

---

[2] Vidya Vrat Agarwal (2021), C# corner, Object oriented programming using C#.Net

when you have to upgrade functionality of an existing type. For instance, all .NET classes inherit from the System. Object class, so a class can hold new functionality as well as use the existing object's class functions and features.

Polymorphism

Polymorphism is a feature that allows one interface to be used for a general class of action. This concept is at times defined as "one interface, multiple actions." The specific action is determined by the exact nature of circumstances.

Reusability

Once a class has been scripted and debugged, it can be shared with other programmers for use in their own programs. This is called reusability. A programmer can use an existing class and, without optimizing it, add additional features if necessary.

This simple one-class console "Hello world" program elaborate many fundamental concepts:

```
using System;
namespace oops
{
    //class definition
    public class SimpleHelloWorld
    {
        //Entry point of the program
        static void Main(string[] args)
        {
            //print Hello world"
```

```
        Console.WriteLine("Hello
World!");
        }
    }
}
```

On line 1, a using directive points to the compiler that this source file refers to classes and constructs declared within the System namespace. Line 6 with the public keyword shows the program accessibility scope for other applications or components.

In line 7, we can see opening curly brace ("{"), which point out the beginning of the SimpleHelloWorld class body. Everything belongs to the class, like fields, properties, and methods appear in the class body between the opening and closing braces. The static keyword in the Main () method states that this method would be implemented without instantiating the class.

Compiling the Program

It is possible to compile a C# program into either an assembly or a module. If the program has one class that includes a Main () method, then it can be compiled directly into an assembly. This file has a ".exe" extension. A program with no main() method can be compiled into a module as in the following:

```
csc/target:module "program name"
```

You can then compile this program by F9 or by simply running the C# command line compiler (csc.exe) against the source file like the following:

```
csc oops.cs
```

Classes and Objects

Classes could be perceived as special types of templates from which you can create objects. Each object has its data and methods to manipulate and access that data. The class defines the data and the functionality that each object of that class can contain.

A class declaration consists of a class header and body. The class header contain modifiers, attributes, and the class keyword. The class body encapsulates the members of the class, which are the data members and member functions. The syntax of a class declaration is as follows:

- Attributes accessibility modifiers class identifier: baselist {body}

Attributes can bring additional context to a class, like adjectives. The following table lists the accessibility keywords:[3]

Keyword	Description
Public	Public class is visible in the current and referencing assembly.
Private	Visible inside current class.
Protected	Visible inside current and derived class.
Internal	Visible inside containing assembly.
Internal protected	Visible inside containing assembly and descendent of the current class.

---

[3] https://www.c-sharpcorner.com/UploadFile/84c85b/object-oriented-pro-gramming-using-C-Sharp-net/, C-sharpcorner

In addition, you can use modifiers to refine the declaration of a class. The list of all modifiers defined in the table are as follows:[4]

Modifier	Description
Sealed	Class can't be inherited by a derived class
Static	Class contains only static members
Unsafe	The class that has some unsafe construct likes pointers.
Abstract	The instance of the class is not created if the Class is abstract.

Multiple Class Declaration

Sometimes circumstances need multiple classes to be declared in a single namespace. Therefore, it is not require to add a separate class to the solution. Instead, you can introduce the new class into the existing program.cs or another one as in the following:[5]

```
using System;
namespace oops
{
    class Program
    {
        public void MainFunction()
        {
            Console.WriteLine("Main class");
        }
        static void Main(string[] args)
```

[4] https://www.c-sharpcorner.com/UploadFile/84c85b/object-oriented-programming-using-C-Sharp-net/, C-sharpcorner
[5] https://www.c-sharpcorner.com/UploadFile/84c85b/object-oriented-programming-using-C-Sharp-net/, C-sharpcorner

```
        {
             //main class instance
             Program obj = new Program();
             obj.MainFunction();

             //other class instace
             demo dObj=new demo();
             dObj.addition();
        }
    }

    class demo
    {
        int x = 10;
        int y = 20;
        int z;

        public void addition()
        {
            z = x + y;
            Console.WriteLine("other class
in Namespace");
            Console.WriteLine(z);
        }
    }
}
```

Here, in this example, we are creating an extra class "demo" in the program.cs file at line 12. And after that, we instanti- ate the demo class with the program class inside the Main() entry in lines 6 to 11.

Partial Classes

Typically, a class will occupy a single file. However, when multiple developers require access to the same class, having the class in multiple files can be helpful. The partial keywords let a class span multiple source files. When compiled, the elements of the partial types are collected into a single assembly.

There are certain rules for defining a partial class as in the following:

- A partial type must have the same accessibility.

- The "partial" keyword precedes each partial type.

- If the partial type is sealed or omitted, then the entire class will be abstract.

In the following example, we include two files, partial-Part1.cs and partialPart2.cs, and declare a partial class, partialclassDemo, in both classes:[6]

```
partialPart1.cs
using System;
namespace oops
{
    public partial class partialclassDemo
    {
        public void method1()
        {
            Console.WriteLine("method from
part1 class");
        }
    }
}
```

---

[6] https://www.c-sharpcorner.com/UploadFile/84c85b/object-oriented-pro-gramming-using-C-Sharp-net/, C-sharpcorner

```
partialPart2.cs
using System;
namespace oops
{
    public partial class partialclassDemo
    {
        public void method2()
        {
            Console.WriteLine("method from
part2 class");
        }
    }
}
```

And finally, we are creating an instance of the partialclass-Demo in the program.cs file as the following:

```
Program.cs
using System;
namespace oops
{
    class Program
    {
        static void Main(string[] args)
        {
            //partial class instance
            partialclassDemo obj = new
partialclassDemo();
            obj.method1();
            obj.method2();
        }
    }
}
```

Static Classes

A static class is declared using the "static" keyword. If the class is declared as static, then the compiler never creates an instance of the class. All the member fields, properties, and functions should be declared as static, and they are accessed by the class name directly, not by a class instance object. To illustrate with an example:

```
using System;
namespace oops
{
    static class staticDemo
    {
        //static fields
        static int x = 10, y;
        //static method
        static void calcute()
        {
            y = x * x;
            Console.WriteLine(y);
        }
        static void Main(string[] args)
        {
            //function calling directly
            staticDemo.calcute();
        }
    }
}
```

Constructor and Destructor

A constructor is a specialized function that is used to initialize fields. A constructor has the same name as the class. Instance constructors are called with the new operator and can't be called in the same manner as other member functions. There are some important rules to constructors that you need to know:

- Classes with no constructor have an implicit constructor called the default constructor, which is parameterless.

- A public constructor allows an object to be created in the current assembly or referencing assembly.

- Only the extern modifier is let on the constructor.

- A constructor returns void but does not have an explicitly declared return type.

- A constructor can have zero or more parameters.

- Classes can have multiple constructors in the form of default, parameter, or both.

The following example reveals one constructor for a customer class:[7]

```
using System;
namespace oops
{
    class customer
    {
        // Member Variables
        public string Name;
```

---

[7] https://www.c-sharpcorner.com/UploadFile/84c85b/object-oriented-programming-using-C-Sharp-net/, C-sharpcorner

```
        //constructor for initializing
fields
        public customer(string fname,
string lname)
        {
            Name= fname +" "+ lname;
        }
        //method for displaying customer
records
        public void AppendData()
        {
            Console.WriteLine(Name);
        }
         //Entry point
        static void Main(string[] args)
        {
            // object instantiation
            customer obj = new
customer("Barack", "Obama");

            //Method calling
            obj.AppendData();
        }
    }
}
```

Once a new statement is implemented, the default constructor is called.

Static Constructor

You create a static constructor to initialize static fields. Static constructors are not called with the new statement at the same time. They are called when the class is first referenced. At the same time, there are certain limitations to the static constructor as in the following:

- Static constructors are parameterless.

- Static constructors can't be overloaded.

- There is no accessibility specified for Static constructors.

In the following example, the customer class has a static constructor that initializes the static field, and this constructor is called when the class is referenced in the Main () at line 26 as in the following:[8]

```
using System;
namespace oops
{
    class customer
    {
        // Member Variables
        static private int x;
        //constuctor for static
initializing fields
        static customer()
        {
            x = 10;
        }
        //method for get  static field
        static public void getData()
```

8 https://www.c-sharpcorner.com/UploadFile/84c85b/object-oriented-programming-using-C-Sharp-net/, C-sharpcorner

```
        {
            Console.WriteLine(x);
        }
         //Entry point
        static void Main(string[] args)
        {
            //static Method calling
            customer.getData();
        }
    }
}
```

Destructors

The purpose of the destructor method is to get rid of unused objects and resources. Destructors are not called during garbage collection. Similar to a constructor, the destructor has the same name as the class, except a destructor is prefixed with a tilde (~). There are some limitations to destructors as in the following:

- Destructors are parameterless.

- A destructor can't be overloaded.

- Destructors are not inherited.

- Destructors can cause performance and efficiency implications.

The following is an implementation of a destructor and dispose method. First of all, we are initializing the fields via constructor, doing some calculations on that data, and sending it to the console. But at line 9, we are introducing the destructor that is calling a Dispose() method to liberate all the resources:[9]

```
using System;
namespace oops
{
    class customer
    {
        // Member Variables
        public int x, y;
        //constuctor for  initializing
fields
        customer()
        {
            Console.WriteLine("Fields
inititalized");
            x = 10;
        }
        //method for get field
        public void getData()
        {
            y = x * x;
            Console.WriteLine(y);
        }
        //method to release resources
explicitly
        public void Dispose()
        {
            Console.WriteLine("Fields
cleaned");
            x = 0;
```

---

9 https://www.c-sharpcorner.com/UploadFile/84c85b/object-oriented-pro-gramming-using-C-Sharp-net/, C-sharpcorner

```
            y = 0;
        }
        //destructor
        ~customer()
        {
            Dispose();
        }
         //Entry point
        static void Main(string[] args)
        {
            //instance created
            customer obj = new customer();

            obj.getData();

        }
    }
}
```

Function Overloading

Function overloading runs multiple implementations of the same function in a class. Overloaded methods have the same name but different specific signature. The number of parameters, types of parameters, or both should not the same. A function can't be overloaded on the basis of a dissimilar return type alone:

```
using System;
namespace oops
{
    class funOverload
    {
        public string name;
```

```csharp
        //overloaded functions
        public void setName(string last)
        {
            name = last;
        }

        public void setName(string first,
string last)
        {
            name = first + "" + last;
        }

        public void setName(string first,
string middle, string last)
        {
            name = first + "" + middle +
"" + last;
        }

        //Entry point
        static void Main(string[] args)
        {
            funOverload obj = new
funOverload();

            obj.setName("barack");
            obj.setName("barack ","
obama ");
            obj.setName("barack
","hussian","obama");

        }
    }
}
```

At lines 3, 4, and 5, we are determining three methods with the same name but with different parameters. In the Main (), you create an instance of the class and call the functions setName() via obj at lines 7, 8, and 9, then intellisense will show forward signatures automatically.

Virtual Methods

By declaring a base class function as virtual, you allow the function to be overridden in any derived class. The idea behind a virtual function is to redefine the implementation of the base class method in the derived class as needed. If a method is virtual in the base class, then we need to give the override keyword in the derived class. Neither member fields nor static functions can be declared as virtual. To demonstrate with an example:

```
using System;
namespace oops
{
    class myBase
    {
        //virtual function
        public virtual void VirtualMethod()
        {
            Console.WriteLine("virtual
method defined in the base class");
        }
    }

    class myDerived : myBase
    {
        // redifing the implementation of
base class method
```

```
        public override void
VirtualMethod()
        {
            Console.WriteLine("virtual
method defined in the Derive class");
        }
    }
    class virtualClass
    {
        static void Main(string[] args)
        {
            // class instance
            new myDerived().
VirtualMethod();
            Console.ReadKey();
        }
    }
}
```

Hiding Methods

If a method with the same signature is declared in both base and derived classes, but the methods are not declared as virtual and overridden, respectively, then the derived class version is said to hide the base class version. In most cases, you would need to override methods rather than hide them. Otherwise, .NET automatically generates a warning.

In the following example, we are defining a VirutalMethod() in the myBase class but not overriding it in the derived class, so in that case, the compiler will generate a warning. The compiler will think that you are hiding the base class method. So to overcome that problem, if you prefix the new keyword in the derived class

method, then the compiler will select the most derived
version method:[10]

```
using System;
namespace oops
{
    class myBase
    {
        //virtual function
        public virtual void VirtualMethod()
        {
            Console.WriteLine("virtual
method defined in the base class");
        }
    }

    class myDerived : myBase
    {
        // hiding the implementation of
base class method
        public new void VirtualMethod()
        {
            Console.WriteLine("virtual
method defined in the Derive class");

            //still access the base class
method
            base.VirtualMethod();
        }
    }
    class virtualClass
```

[10] https://www.c-sharpcorner.com/UploadFile/84c85b/object-oriented-pro-
gramming-using-C-Sharp-net/, C-sharpcorner

```
    {
        static void Main(string[] args)
        {
            // class instance
            new myDerived().VirtualMethod();
            Console.ReadKey();
        }
    }
}
```

Abstract Classes

C# allows both classes and functions to be declared using the abstract keyword. You can't make an instance of an abstract class. An abstract member has its own signature, but does not have a function body, and they should be overridden in any non-abstract derived class. Abstract classes exist primarily for inheritance. Member functions, properties, and indexers can be abstract. A class with one or more abstract members must be abstract as well. However, static members can't be abstract.

In the following example, we are declaring an abstract class Employees with a method displayData() that does not have an implementation. Then we implement the displayData() body in the derived class. One point to be mentioned here is that we have to prefix the abstract method with the override keyword in the derived class:[11]

```
using System;
namespace oops
{
    //abstract class
    public abstract class Employees
```

---

[11] https://www.c-sharpcorner.com/UploadFile/84c85b/object-oriented-programming-using-C-Sharp-net/, C-sharpcorner

```
    {
        //abstract method with no
implementation
        public abstract void displayData();
    }
    //derived class
    public class test: Employees
    {
        //abstract class method
implementation
        public override void displayData()
        {
            Console.WriteLine("Abstract
class method");
        }
    }
    class abstractClass
    {
        static void Main(string[] args)
        {
            // class instance
            new test().displayData();
        }
    }
}
```

Sealed Classes

Sealed classes are the opposite of abstract classes. While abstract classes are inherited and are refined in the derived class, sealed classes cannot be inherited. You can create an instance of a sealed class.

Let's say you are a developer of a class library, and some of the classes in the class library are extensible, but other classes are not extensible, so in that case, those classes are marked as sealed:

```
using System;
namespace oops
{
    sealed class SealedClass
    {
        void myfunv();
    }

    public class test : SealedClass //
wrong. will give a compilation error
    {
    }
}
```

Interface
An interface is a set of related functions that must be implemented in a derived class. Interfaces are similar to abstract classes. First, both types must be inherited; second, you cannot create an instance of either. Although there are several differences as in the following;

- An Abstract class can contain some implementations, but an interface can't.

- An Interface can only inherit other interfaces, but abstract classes can inherit from other classes and interfaces.

- An Abstract class can contain constructors and destructors, but an interface can't.

- An Abstract class contains fields, but interfaces don't.

At the same time, with an interface, the derived type still can inherit from another type, and interfaces are more straightforward than abstract classes. Take a look at the following example:[12]

```
using System;
namespace oops
{
    // interface
    public interface xyz
    {
        void methodA();
        void methodB();
    }

    // interface method implementation
    class test : xyz
    {
        public void methodA()
        {

Console.WriteLine("methodA");
        }
        public void methodB()
        {

Console.WriteLine("methodB");
        }
    }
    class interfaceDemo
    {
```

---

[12] https://www.c-sharpcorner.com/UploadFile/84c85b/object-oriented-pro-gramming-using-C-Sharp-net/, C-sharpcorner

```
        static void Main(string[] args)
        {
            test obj = new test();
            obj.methodA();
            obj.methodB();
        }
    }
}
```

ENCAPSULATION AND INHERITANCE

Encapsulation is defined as the wrapping up of data under a single unit. It is the mechanism that stitches together code and the data it manipulates. Differently, encapsulation is a protective shield that stops the data from being accessed by the code outside this shield.

Technically in encapsulation, the variables or data of a class are hidden from any other class and can be obtained only through any member function of its class in which they are declared.

Encapsulation can be attained by: Declaring all the variables in the class as private and using C# Properties in the class to set and get the values of variables. For example:[13]

```
// C# program to illustrate encapsulation
using System;

public class DemoEncap {

    // private variables declared
    // these can only be accessed by
    // public methods of class
```

---

[13] https://www.geeksforgeeks.org/c-sharp-encapsulation/, geeksforgeeks

```csharp
private String studentName;
private int studentAge;

// using accessors to get and
// set the value of studentName
public String Name
{

    get
    {
        return studentName;
    }

    set
    {
        studentName = value;
    }

}

// using accessors to get and
// set the value of studentAge
public int Age
{

    get
    {
        return studentAge;
    }

    set
    {
        studentAge = value;
    }
```

```csharp
    }

      }

// Driver Class
class GFG {

    // Main Method
    static public void Main()
    {

        // creating object
        DemoEncap obj = new DemoEncap();

        // calls set accessor of the
property Name,
        // and pass "Ankita" as value of the
        // standard field 'value'
        obj.Name = "Ankita";

        // calls set accessor of the
property Age,
        // and pass "21" as value of the
        // standard field 'value'
        obj.Age = 21;

        // Displaying values of the
variables
        Console.WriteLine("Name: " + obj.
Name);
        Console.WriteLine("Age: " + obj.
Age);
    }
}
```

- **Output:**
  - Name: Ankita
  - Age: 21

In the above program, the class DemoEncap is encapsulated as the variables are declared as private. In order to access these private variables, we are using the Name and Age accessors which contain the get and set method to retrieve and set the values of private fields. Accessors are defined as public so that they can access in other classes.

Advantages of Encapsulation

- **Data Hiding:** The user will have no idea about the inner implementation of the class.[14] It will not be visible to the user that how the class is stored values in the variables.

- **Increased Flexibility:** You can make the variables of the class read-only or write-only depending on our requirement. If we wish to make the variables read-only then we have to only use Get Accessor in the code. If we wish to make the variables write-only, then we have to only use Set Accessor.

- **Reusability:** Encapsulation also improves the reusability and is easy to change with new requirements.

- **Testing code is easy:** Encapsulated code is easy to test for unit testing.

---

[14] Encapsulation in Java (2021), GeeksforGeeks

Inheritance

We have already discussed inheritance previously and addressed it as the process of acquiring all the properties of one class into another class. Specifically, there are two classes named as base class and derived class. The base class acts as a parent class and the properties or methods of this class we want to inherit to another class.

The derived class is perceived as the child class that is activated to inherit the properties and methods of the base class or parent class. It allows to reuse the same code again, without having to define the same properties all over again.

Types of Inheritance in C#

There are different types of Inheritance in C#:

1. **Single Level Inheritance:** In Single inheritance, there is only one base class and one derived class. It means the child class will inherit the properties of the parent class and use them. For example:[15]

```
class BaseClass
{
public void hello()
{
Console.WriteLine("Parent's Hello
Method");
}
}
class ChildClass : BaseClass
{
```

---

[15] https://www.educba.com/inheritance-in-csharp/, Educba

```
public void World()
{
Console.WriteLine("Child's World
Method");
}
}
```

2. **Multilevel Inheritance:** In this type of inheritance, there is only one base class, and multiple derived classes are available. If a class is created by using another derived class is known as multilevel inheritance. Example:

```
class BaseClass
{
public void hello()
{
Console.WriteLine("Parent's Hello
Method");
}
}
class ChildClass : BaseClass
{
public void World()
{
Console.WriteLine("Child's World
Method");
}
}
class SecondChildClass : ChildClass
{
public void Hi()
{
}
}
```

3. **Multiple Inheritance:** In this type of inheritance, this can be achieved with the help of multiple interfaces, not with a class. In simple words, C# does not support multiple inheritances, but if you want to achieve it, then it can be achieved with the help of interfaces only. For example:

   • Interface A {}

   • Interface B {}

   • Class C: A, B {}

4. **Hierarchical Inheritance:** In this type of inheritance, there is one parent class, and the other derived classes inherit the same parent class to achieve this inheritance. To illustrate:[16]

```
class BaseClass
{
public void hello()
{
Console.WriteLine("Parent's Hello
Method");
}
}
class ChildClass : BaseClass
{
public void World()
{
Console.WriteLine("Child's World
Method");
}
```

---

[16] https://www.educba.com/inheritance-in-csharp/, Educba

```
}
class SecondChildClass : BaseClass
{
public void Hi()
{
}
}
```

Advantages of Inheritance in C#

Below are the main advantages of Inheritance:

- It reduces code redundancy.

- It also reduces the size of the source code and file.

- It helps in providing the extensibility to code.

- The code is easy to manage as it divided into classes of the base class and child class.

- Private members are not accessed in derived class when base class members are inherited by the derived class.

- It does not support multiple inheritances but can be achieved through interfaces.

- It helps in achieving the polymorphism that allows an object to represent more than one type.

Following are the essential features of Inheritance:[17]

- Inheritance can be used to prevent the direct instantiation of the class, and to achieve this, the abstract keyword has been used.

---

[17] https://www.educba.com/inheritance-in-csharp/, Educba

- The members of the base class can be accessed in the derived class except for private key members.

- The members of the base class can be inherited in the derived class except for the constructor and destructor as well.

- In C#, the virtual methods of a base class need to use an override keyword in the derived class.

- In C#, to prevent the inheritance of the class that can be declared with the sealed keyword.

- If the inherited members need to be hidden with the same name and signature in the derived class, then that method needs to be defined with the new keyword.

Why Use Inheritance and How It Makes It Easy to Work?

It makes it easy to work on because it helps in avoiding the confusion of method calling from which class method is getting called. It makes the code reusability and makes the file lighter in weight with fewer lines of source code. This makes the code less redundant and more flexible to use in different classes. It keeps the structure of the program that helps in reading the code easily.

CONCLUSION

To summarize, inheritance is the most widely used concept of OOP in all the OOPs based languages and so as in C#. It helps the developer to complete many things and makes the code more readable and approachable.

Polymorphism is the other great concept that can be achieved with the help of Inheritance only. Most of the issues have been resolved with these two concepts going hand in hand.

Inheritance needs to be used very carefully as if the data members are not properly used and the memory is allocated to them, then it affects the performance of the application. At the same time, there are various levels of inheritance that are used in programming or developing an application. It can be utilized in any type of application, like web-based or desktop-based applications. It typically depends on the developer how and where to use inheritance as it gives a lot of flexibility, features, and helps to achieve specific code goals.

CHAPTER 6

Generics in C#

IN THIS CHAPTER

- ➤ What are Generics
- ➤ Generic Types and Methods
- ➤ Covariance and Contravariance in Generics

We have covered object-oriented programming (OOP) and its implementation in the last chapter, and now, we will discuss Generics and its types and methods. The word "Generic" means "not determined." Put simply, it is a generic form of representing an element. Generic solutions are obviously the need of the hour in a fast-changing world of software. What we need is a comprehensive solution that can simply sort out multiple problems of similar nature with no alteration to the solution.

DOI: 10.1201/9781003214779-6

Similarly, we may witness multiple data types in the same way while the code is being developed. For example, we have a bunch of strings in a code. In it, we perform certain kinds of operations by using the built-in functionality of the list. Not only that, there is a list of integers in the code, where we have the absolute freedom to run the operations using the built-in list functionality.

So imagine there is a need to implement a user-defined functionality, and it has to be familiar and work with all the primitive and user-defined data types. So there is a need to develop a generic class similar to List (that comes with C# collections), and it should include methods like the ones that are in lists (Add, AddRange, Where, etc.). And the methods have got to work with the same set of data types as the new class.

So, how to create a user-defined class with data types assigned at run time and executes methods that are part of it? C# comes with a feature called Generics provides us an answer to this.

WHAT ARE GENERICS

Generic is a class that lets the user define classes and methods with the placeholder. Generics were incorporated into version 2.0 of the C# language. The fundamental idea behind using Generic is to let type (Integer, String, … etc., and user-defined types) be a parameter to classes, methods, and interfaces. A main limitation of collections is the absence of productive type checking. This actually means that you can put any object in a collection as all classes in the C# programming language stick out from the object base class. This, in effect, compromises type safety and contradicts the basic definition of C# as a type-safe language. Not only that, using collections comprises a significant performance overhead in the form of implicit and explicit type casting that is essential to add or retrieve objects from a collection.

To squarely address the type safety issue, the .NET framework gives generics to create structures, classes, methods, and interfaces that have placeholders for the types they use. Generics are usually used to create type-safe collections for both reference and value types. The .NET framework gives an extensive set of interfaces and classes in the System.Collections.Generic namespace for implementing generic collections.

Characteristics of Generics

Generics is a technique that enhance your programs in many ways, such as:

- It allows you in code performance, reuse, and type safety.

- You can create your own generic methods, classes, interfaces, and delegates.

- You can create generic collection classes. The .NET Framework class library includes many new generic collection classes in System.Collections.Generic namespace.

- You will get information on the types used in generic data types at run-time.

There are some important characteristics of Generic types that make them special to the conventional nongeneric type as follows:

- Type Safety.

- Performance.

- Binary Code reuse.

Type Safety

One of the most important features of Generics is Type Safety. In the case of the nongeneric ArrayList class, if objects are used, any type can be attach to the collections that can sometimes result in a great problem. The following example point out that adding a, string integer, and object to the collection of an ArrayList type:

```
ArrayList obj = new ArrayList();
obj.Add(50);
obj.Add("Dog");
obj.Add(new TestClass());
```

Now, if the collection is going through the foreach statement using integer elements, the compiler accepts the code, but because all the elements in the collection are not an integer, a runtime exception occurs:

```
foreach(int i in obj)
{
    Console.WriteLine(i);
}
```

The rule of thumb in programming is that errors should be detected as early as possible. With the generic class Test<T>, the generic type T defines what types are allowed. With the definition of Test<int>, only an integer type can be added to the collection. The compiler doesn't compile the code because the Add() method has invalid arguments as follows:

```
Test<int> obj = new Test<int>();
obj.Add(50);
obj.Add("Dog");              //compiler error
obj.Add(new TestClass());  //compiler error
```

Performance

Another key component of Generics is its performance. Applying value types with nongeneric collection classes typically follows up with boxing and unboxing overhead once a value type is translated to reference type.

In the next example, the ArrayList class stores objects, and the Add() method is set to keep some integer type argument. So an integer type is boxed. When the value from ArrayList is read using the foreach statement, unboxing activates:[1]

```
ArrayList  obj = new ArrayList();
obj.Add(50);    //boxing- convert value
type to reference type
int x= (int)obj[0]; //unboxing
foreach(int i in obj)
{
   Console.WriteLine(i);   // unboxing
}
```

---

[1] https://resources.infosecinstitute.com/topic/generics/, infosecinstitute

Generics are faster than other collections such as ArrayList.

Instead of using objects, a Generics type of the TestClass<T> class is defined as an int, so an int type is used inside the class that isproduced dynamically from the compiler.[2] Therefore boxing and unboxing no longer occurs as in the following:

```
TestClass<int> obj = new TestClass<int>();
obj.Add(50);     //No boxing
int x= obj[0]; // No unboxing
foreach(int i in obj)
{
   Console.WriteLine(i);    //No unboxing
}
```

Binary Code Reuse

Generics gives a kind of source code protection. A Generic class can be defined once and can be instantiated with many different types. Generics can be defined in one CLR supported language and used from another .NET language. The following TestClass<T> is instantiated with an int and string types:

```
TestClass<int> obj = new TestClass<int>();
obj.Add(50);

TestClass<string> obj1 = new
TestClass<string>();
Obj1.Add("hello");
```

---

[2] Vidya Vrat Agarwal (2020), C# corner, *Generics in C#*

Generic Methods

While most developers will usually use the existing generic types within the base class libraries, it is certainly possible to build your own generic members and custom generic types.

The main objective of this example is to build a swap method that can operate on any possible data type (value-based or reference-based) using a single type parameter. Due to the nature of swapping algorithms, the incoming parameters will be sent by reference via ref keyword:

```
using System;
using System.Collections.Generic;

namespace GenericApp
{
    class Program
    {
        //Generic method
        static void Swap<T>(ref T a, ref T b)
        {
            T temp;
            temp = a;
            a = b;
            b = temp;
        }
        static void Main(string[] args)
        {
            // Swap of two integers.
            int a = 40, b = 60;
            Console.WriteLine("Before swap:
{0}, {1}", a, b);
            Swap<int>(ref a, ref b);
            Console.WriteLine("After
swap: {0}, {1}", a, b);
```

```
                Console.ReadLine();
        }


}
}
```

Generic Class and Methods

C# also have classes and methods not made for a specific type but can be used with any general type.

We normally use <> brackets for this purpose. Suppose we have set a class or method with <T> and run each operation on T inside the method or the class. And we added an integer while calling it—<int>, then the T inside the class or the method will be changed to take int during the time of compilation. Let's look at generic classes here:

```
using System;
class Generic<T>
{
  private T genericVariable;
  public Generic(T genericValue)
  {
    this.genericVariable = genericValue;
  }
  public void Display()
  {
    Console.WriteLine(this.
genericVariable);
  }
}
class Test
{
  static void Main(string[] args)
```

```
  {
    Generic<int> g = new Generic<int>(5);
    Generic<string> g1 = new
Generic<string>("CodesDope");
    g.Display();
    g1.Display();
  }
}
```

- **Output:** CodesDope

In the above example, we have defined a generic class—class Generic<T>. And withing the class, we have treated T as normal data and declared a variable of type T—private T genericVariable.

Also, in the constructor, we are taking a variable of type T—public Generic (T genericValue). Later make sure that the type of T will be determined while making the object of the class.

Generic<int> g = new Generic<int>(5); → Here, the type of T is an integer. So, T will become int inside the definition of the class.

Generic<string> g1 = new Generic<string>("CodesD ope"); → In the object g1, T is string. So, T will become a string inside the definition of the class.

After implementation of Generic<int> g = new Generic<int>(5); Generic class would be something like:[3]

```
class Generic
{
  private int genericVariable;
  public Generic(int genericValue)
```

---

[3] https://www.codesdope.com/course/c-sharp-generics/, Codesdope

```
  {
    this.genericVariable = genericValue;
  }
  public void Display()
  {
    Console.WriteLine(this.genericVariable);
  }
}
```

Let's take one more example:

```
using System;
class Generic<T, U>
{
  public T GenericVariableFirst
  {
    get;
    set;
  }
  public U GenericVariableSecond
  {
    get;
    set;
  }
}
class Test
{
  static void Main(string[] args)
  {
    Generic<int, string> g = new Generic<int,
string>();
    g.GenericVariableFirst = 10;
    g.GenericVariableSecond = "abc";
    Console.WriteLine(g.GenericVariableFirst);
```

```
    Console.WriteLine(g.
GenericVariableSecond);
  }
}
10
abc
```

In this example, we have defined our class to work on class Generic<T, U>. Also, while making the object, we have set T as int and U as string—Generic<int, string> g.

C# Constraint

We used a placeholder T in the above examples, and this placeholder can be of any type. In C#, we can also constraint the type of placeholder using the where keyword. Suppose we have defined a class as:

class ClassName<T> where T: class

In this case, T can only be a reference type like class, string, etc. If we try with something else, we will get an error.

Here, class in where T: class means T/can be a reference type. Let's look at the table given below for another type of constraint.

Constraint	Description
Class	Must be reference type
Struct	Must be value type
new()	Must have a public parameterless constructor
BaseClassName	Must be derivied from BaseClassName class
InterfaceName	Must implement InterfaceName interface.
U	Must be or derive from the argument supplied for U.

Now let's illustrate these types with the following example:

```
using System;
class Generic<T> where T: class
{
  public T GenericVariable
  {
    get;
    set;
  }
}
class Test
{
  static void Main(string[] args)
  {
    Generic<int> g = new Generic<int>();
    g.GenericVariable = 10;
    Console.WriteLine(g.GenericVariable);
  }
}
```

In the example above, we constrained the placeholder to take only references type using class, and we tried to make an object with an integer for the placeholder. Since int is a value type, we got errors while compiling the code.

Let's try with a reference type.

```
using System;
class Generic<T> where T: class
{
  public T GenericVariable
  {
```

```
    get;
    set;
  }
}

class Test
{
  static void Main(string[] args)
  {
    Generic<string> g = new
Generic<string>();

    g.GenericVariable = "CodesDope";

    Console.WriteLine(g.GenericVariable);
  }
}
```

In this example, we tried with a string which is a reference type, and thus code compiled successfully.

C# Multiple Constraints

We can also have multiple constraints. Let's take an example:

```
using System;
class Generic<T, U> where T: class where
U: struct
{
  public T GenericVariableFirst
  {
    get;
    set;
  }
```

```csharp
  public U GenericVariableSecond
  {
    get;
    set;
  }
}
class Test
{
  static void Main(string[] args)
  {
    Generic<string, int> g = new
Generic<string, int>();
    g.GenericVariableFirst = "CodesDope";
    g.GenericVariableSecond = 10;
    Console.WriteLine(g.GenericVariableFirst);
    Console.WriteLine(g.
GenericVariableSecond);
  }
}
```

In addition, you can derive a generic class to make sub-classes of it. To illustrate with an example:

```csharp
using System;
class Generic<T>
{
  public T GenericVariable
  {
    get;
    set;
  }
}
class Derived: Generic<int>
{
```

```
}
class Test
{
  static void Main(string[] args)
  {
    Derived d = new Derived();
  }
}
```

In this example, we have made a subclass and passed int during delivering it .class delivered: generic<int>.

GENERIC TYPES AND METHODS

Generic types and methods are visually distinguishing because they always have angle brackets (< and >) after the name. These include a comma-separated list of arguments or parameters. The same argument/parameter distinction applies here as with methods: The declaration specifies a list of parameters. When you decide to apply the method or type, you deliver arguments for those parameters. So List<T> defines a single type parameter, T, and List<int> supplies a type argument, int, for that parameter.

Type parameters can be named any way you like, within the usual constraints for identifiers in C#. There's a usual but not universal convention of using T when there's only one parameter. For multiparameter generics, you tend to see somewhat more descriptive names.

Generic Types

Classes, interfaces, and structs can all be generic. The syntax for structs and interfaces is similar: The type name is followed immediately by a type parameter list. Defining a generic class:

```
public class NamedContainer<T>
{
    public NamedContainer(T item, string
name)
    {
        Item = item;
        Name = name;
    }

    public T Item { get; }
    public string Name { get; }
}
```

Inside the body of the class, we can use the type parameter T anywhere you would normally see a type name. In this case, we have used it as the type of a constructor argument and also the Item property. We could define fields of type T too.[4]

The class in the example above defines, like any generic type, not a complete type. A generic type declaration is not constrained, meaning that type parameters must be filled in to produce a complete type. When type arguments are supplied, the result is sometimes called a constructed type.

You can use a constructed generic type anywhere you would use a normal type. For example, you can use them as the types for method parameters and return values, fields, or properties. You can even use one as a type argument for another generic type.

---

[4] Ian Grifiths (2019), Programming in c# 8.0, Generics -programming c# 8.0 -O'Reilly

```
// …where a, and b come from in the
Example.
var namedInts = new
List<NamedContainer<int>>() { a, b};
var namedNamedItem = new NamedContainer<Na
medContainer<int>>(a, "Wrapped");
```

Each different type we supply as an argument to
NamedContainer<T> constructs a distinct type. This basically means that NamedContainer<int> is a different type
than NamedContainer<string>. That's why there's no con-
flict in using NamedContainer<int> as the type argument
for another NamedContainer as the final line of Example
illustrates.

Since each different set of type arguments has a distinct type, in most cases, there is no implied compatibility
between different forms of the same generic type. You cannot possibly turn a NamedContainer<int> into a variable
of type NamedContainer<string> or vice versa. It makes
sense that those two types are irreconcilable because int
and string are quite different types.

Yet what if we used the object as a type argument?
You can put almost anything in an object variable. If
you include a method with a parameter of type object, it
would be acceptable to pass a string, so you might expect a
method that takes a NamedContainer<object> to be compatible with a NamedContainer<string>. That won't work,
but some generic types (expressly, interfaces, and delegates)
can state that they require this kind of compatibility relationship. The mechanisms that support this (called covariance and contravariance) are closely related to the type
system's inheritance mechanisms.

The number of type parameters forms certain part of generic type's identity. This makes it possible to introduce multiple types with the same name as long as they have different type parameters. Meaning that you could define a generic class called, say, Operation<T>, and then another class, Operation<T1, T2>, and also Operation<T1, T2, T3>, and so on, all in the same namespace, without introducing any ambiguity. When using these types, it's clear from the number of arguments which type was meant— Operation<int> uses the first, while Operation<string, double> uses the second, for instance. And following the same pattern, a nongeneric Operation class would be very much distinct from generic types of the same name.

My NamedContainer<T> example doesn't affect instances of its type argument, T—it never invokes any methods or uses any properties or other members of T. All it does is accept a T as a constructor argument, which it stores away for later retrieval. This is also true of many generic types in the .NET class library—we have mentioned some collection classes, which are all variations on the same theme of including data for later retrieval. The reason for this is quite simple: A generic class can find itself working with any type so that it can assume little about its type arguments. However, you can change it and specify constraints for your type of argument.

Constraints

C# let you to state that a type of argument must fulfill specific requirements. For example, suppose you want to be able to create new instances of the type on demand. Example shows a simple class that provides deferred construction – it makes an instance available through a static property. Still, it does not attempt to construct that instance until the first time you read the property. The below example shows how to create a new instance of a parameterized type:

```
public static class Deferred<T>
    where T : new()
{
    private static T _instance;

    public static T Instance
    {
        get
        {
            if (_instance == null)
            {
_instance = new T();
            }
            return _instance;
        }
    }
}
```

In order to activate this class, you are expected to construct an instance of whatever type is supplied as the argument for T. The get accessor uses the new keyword. Since it passes no arguments, it requires T to give a parameterless constructor. But not all types do, so if we try to use a type without a suitable constructor as the argument for Deferred<T> the compiler will inevitably reject it. Constraints come before the class's opening brace, and they start with the where keyword. The new() constraint in the Example above states that T is required to supply a zero-argument constructor.

Type Constraints

You can constrain the argument for a type parameter to match a particular type. For instance, you could use this to demand that the argument type runs a certain interface. Let's take a look at this syntax:

```
using System;
using System.Collections.Generic;

public class GenericComparer<T> : IComparer<T>
    where T : IComparable<T>
{
    public int Compare(T x, T y)
    {
        return x.CompareTo(y);
    }
}
```

Let's briefly explain the purpose of this example before describing how it takes advantage of a type constraint. This class acts as a link between two styles of value comparison that you'll find in .NET. Some data types have their own comparison logic, but it can sometimes be more useful for comparison to be a separate function implemented in its class. These two styles are represented by the IComparable<T> and IComparer<T> interfaces, which are both parts of the class library. The interface defines a single Compare method that takes two arguments and returns either a negative number, 0, or a positive number if the first argument is less than, equal to, or greater than the second. IComparable<T> is very similar, but its CompareTo method takes just a single argument because, with this interface, you are asking an instance to compare itself to some other instance.

Some of the .NET class library's collection classes ask you to provide an IComparer<T> to support ordering operations such as sorting. They use the model in which a separate object compares because this provide two advantages over the IComparable<T> model. First, it allows you to use data types that don't implement IComparable<T>. Then, it let you access different sorting orders. So IComparer<T> is the more flexible model. However, if you use a data type that implements IComparable<T>, just use the .NET feature designed for this very scenario: Comparer<T>.Default. If T implements IComparable<T>, that property will return an IComparer<T> that does precisely what you want. So in practice, you wouldn't have to write the code in the example above, because Microsoft has already scripted it for you.

At the same time, interface constraints are somewhat unusual. If a method needs a particular argument to implement a specific interface, you wouldn't normally need a generic type constraint. You can just use that interface as the argument type so it won't compile:

```
public class GenericComparer<T> : IComparer<T>
{
    public int Compare(IComparable<T> x, T y)
    {
        return x.CompareTo(y);
    }
}
```

The compiler will complain that we have not implemented the IComparer<T> interface's Compare method. Example above has a Compare method, but its signature is wrong—that first argument should be a T.

```
public class GenericComparer<T> :
IComparer<T>
{
    public int Compare(T x, T y)
    {
        return x.CompareTo(y);
    }
}
```

That will also fail to compile because the compiler can't find that CompareTo method we are trying to use. The constraint for T in Example enables the compiler to know what that method really is.

Type constraints don't have to be interfaces. You can use any type. For example, you can constrain a particular argument to always derive from a specific base class. Moreover, you can also define one parameter's constraint in terms of another type parameter:

```
public class Foo<T1, T2>
    where T1 : T2
. . .
```

Type constraints are pretty specific—they require either a special inheritance relationship or the implementation of specific interfaces. However, you can define slightly fewer particular constraints.

Reference Type Constraints

Basically, you can constrain a type argument to be a reference type. You just put the keyword class instead of a type name. If you are using C# 8.0, and are in an enabled nullable annotation context, the meaning of this annotation changes: It requires the type argument to be a non-nullable reference type. In case you also specify the class, the type argument can either become nullable or a non-nullable reference type. Standard syntax:

```
public class Bar<T>
    where T : class
...
```

This constraint prevents using value types such as int, double, or any struct as the type argument. Its presence enables your code to do three things that would not otherwise be possible. First, it means that you can add code that tests whether variables of the relevant type are null. Second, you can use it as the operator's target type. This is just a variation on the first feature—the as keyword requires a reference type because it can produce a null result.

The third feature that a reference type constraint allow is the capacity to use certain other generic types. It's often useful for generic code to apply one of its type arguments as an argument for another generic type. If that other type specifies a constraint, you'll need to put the same constraint on your type parameter. So if some other type specifies a class constraint, this might need you to constrain one of your arguments in the same way.

Of course, this does raise the question of why the type you're using needs the constraint in the first place. The reason for it is that sometimes, you just need a type argument to be a reference type—there are situations in which a generic method might be able to compile without a class constraint, but it will not work correctly if used with a value type.

Tests that create an instance of the class we are testing and that also need one or more fake objects to stand in for real objects with which the object under test wants to interact. Using these stand-ins minimize the amount of code any single test has to exercise and can make it easier to verify the behavior of the object being tested:

```
using Microsoft.VisualStudio.TestTools.
UnitTesting;
using Moq;

public class TestBase<TSubject, TFake>
    where TSubject : new()
    where TFake : class
{
    public TSubject Subject { get; private
set; }
    public Mock<TFake> Fake { get; private
set; }

    [TestInitialize]
    public void Initialize()
    {
        Subject = new TSubject();
        Fake = new Mock<TFake>();
    }
}
```

There are various ways to build mock objects for test purposes. You could just write new classes that implement the

same interface as your real objects, but third-party libraries can generate them. One such library is called Moq,
and that's where the Mock<T> class in the Example above
comes from. It's capable of generating a fake implementation of any interface or any nonsealed class. It will also offer
empty implementations of all members by default, and you
can configure more interesting behaviors if necessary.

Moreover, Moq generates a type at runtime, and if T is
an interface, that generated type will implement it, whereas
if T is a class, the generated type will derive from it.

To put it simply, if you want to use one of your own type
parameters as the type argument for a generic that specifies a constraint, you'll need to specify the same constraint
on your type parameter.

Value Type Constraints

Just as you can constrain a type argument to be a reference
type, you can also constrain it to be a value type. Example
above shows that the syntax is similar to that for a reference type constraint but with the struct keyword. Let's take
a look at the example of constraint requiring a value type:

```
public class Quux<T>
    where T : struct
. . .
```

Before now, we've seen the struct keyword only in the context of custom value types, but despite how it looks, this
constraint allow any of the built-in numeric types such as
int, as well as custom structs.

.NET's Nullable<T> type imposes this constraint.
The only reason this type exists is to provide nullability

for types that would not otherwise be able to hold a null value. So it only makes sense to use this with a value type – reference type variables can already be set to null without needing this wrapper. The value type constraint stops you from using Nullable<T> with types for which it is unnecessary.

Value Types Down with Unmanaged Constraints

It is also possible to specify unmanaged as a constraint, which requires that the type argument be a value type, but also that it contains no references. Not only does this mean that all of the type's fields must be value types, but the type of each field must, in turn, include only fields that are value types, and so on down. In practice, this does means that all the actual data needs to be either one of a fixed set of built-in types or an enum type. This is mainly because types that match the unmanaged constraint can be passed safely and efficiently to unmanaged code.

Not Null Constraints

C# 8.0 brings a new constraint type, not null, which is available if you add the further nullable references feature. If you do this, then either value types or non-nullable reference types are allowed.

Other Special Type Constraints

It is sometimes convenient to constrain type arguments to be one of these kinds of types. There's no unique trick to this: you can simply use type constraints. All delegate types derive from System.Delegate, and all enumeration types derive from System.Enum. Therefore, you can write a type constraint requiring a type argument to derive from either:[5]

```
public class RequireDelegate<T>
    where T : Delegate
{
}

public class RequireEnum<T>
    where T : Enum
{
}
```

Multiple Constraints

If you'd like to impose multiple constraints for a single type argument, you can just put them in a list. However, there are a few ordering restrictions: If you have a reference or value type constraint, the class or struct keyword must come first in the list. If the new() constraint is present, it must be last:

```
public class Spong<T>
    where T : IEnumerable<T>, IDisposable,
new()
. . .
```

When your type has multiple type parameters, you add a clause for each type parameter you want to constrain.

[5] https://www.oreilly.com/library/view/programming-c-80/9781492056805/ch04.html, O'Reilly

Type Inference

The C# compiler is often used to infer the type arguments for a generic method. Standard example of Generic method type argument inference look like this:

```
int[] values = { 1, 2, 3 };
int last = GetLast(values);
```

When provided with this sort of ordinary-looking method call, if there's no nongeneric method of that name available, the compiler will start looking for other generic methods.

Nevertheless, it gets more complicated with more intricate cases. The C# specification has about six pages dedicated to the type inference algorithm. Still, it's all to support one purpose: letting you omit type arguments when they would be redundant. By the way, type inference is always running at compile time, so it's based on the static type of the method arguments.

APIs that make extensive use of generics explicitly listing every type of argument can make the code very hard to remember, so it is common to depend on type inference. And if you use anonymous types, type argument inference becomes necessary because it is impossible to supply the type arguments explicitly.

COVARIANCE AND CONTRAVARIANCE IN GENERICS

Covariance and contravariance refer to the ability to use a more derived type (more specific) or a less derived type (less specific) than initially specified. Generic type parameters support covariance and contravariance to give greater flexibility in assigning and using generic types.

Covariant type parameters allow you to make assignments that look much like ordinary Polymorphism, as shown in the following code:

```
IEnumerable<Derived> d = new
List<Derived>();
IEnumerable<Base> b = d;
```

The List<T> class implements the IEnumerable<T> interface, so List<Derived> (List(Of Derived) in Visual Basic) implements IEnumerable<Derived>. The covariant type parameter does the rest.

Contravariance, on the other hand, seems counterintuitive. The below example creates a delegate of type Action<Base> (Action(Of Base) in Visual Basic) and then allocate that delegate to a variable of type Action<Derived>:[6]

```
Action<Base> b = (target) => { Console.
WriteLine(target.GetType().Name); };
Action<Derived> d = b;
d(new Derived());
```

It might seem backward, but it is type-safe code that compiles and runs. The lambda expression matches the delegate it's assigned to, so it defines a method that takes one parameter of type Base and has no return value. The resulting delegate can be assigned to a variable of type Action<Derived> because the type parameter T of the Action<T> delegate is contravariant. The code is type-safe because T specifies a parameter type. When the delegate of type Action<Base>

---

[6] https://docs.microsoft.com/en-us/dotnet/standard/generics/covariance-and-contravariance, Microsoft

is invoked as if it were a delegate of type Action<Derived>, its argument must be of type Derived. This argument can always be passed safely to the underlying method, because the method's parameter is of type Base.[7]

In general, a covariant type parameter can be applied as the return type of a delegate, and contravariant type parameters can be seen as parameter types.

Basically, both covariance and contravariance are referred to as variance. A generic type parameter that is not set as covariant or contravariant is referred to as invariant. A summary of facts about variance in the common language runtime:

- Variant type parameters are restricted to generic interface and generic delegate types.

- A generic interface or generic delegate type can have both covariant and contravariant type parameters.

- Variance applies only to reference types; if you specify a value type for a variant type parameter, that type parameter is invariant for the resulting constructed type.

- Variance does not apply to delegate combination. That is, given two delegates of types Action<Derived> and Action<Base> (Action(Of Derived) and Action(Of Base) in Visual Basic), you cannot combine the second delegate with the first, although the result would be type safe.

---

[7] Billwagner et al. (2017), Microsoft, Covariance and contravariance in generics

- • Variance allows the second delegate to be assigned to a variable of type Action<Derived>, but delegates can combine only if their types match precisely.

Now let's take a look at the following example to elaborate covariant type parameters. The example defines two types: Base has a static method named PrintBases that takes an IEnumerable<Base> (IEnumerable(Of Base) in Visual Basic) and prints the elements. Derived inherits from Base. The example creates an empty List<Derived> (List(Of Derived) in Visual Basic) and demonstrates that this type can be passed to PrintBases and assigned to a variable of type IEnumerable<Base> without casting. List<T> implements IEnumerable<T>, which has a single covariant type parameter:

```
using System;
using System.Collections.Generic;
class Base
{
    public static void
PrintBases(IEnumerable<Base> bases)
    {
        foreach(Base b in bases)
        {
Console.WriteLine(b);
        }
    }
}
class Derived : Base
{
    public static void Main()
    {
```

```
List<Derived> dlist = new List<Derived>();
        Derived.PrintBases(dlist);
IEnumerable<Base> bIEnum = dlist;
    }
}
```

Generic Interfaces with Contravariant Type Parameters

Several generic interfaces have contravariant type parameters; for instance: IComparer<T>, IComparable<T>, and IEqualityComparer<T>. These interfaces have only contravariant type parameters, so the type parameters are used only as parameter types in the members of the interfaces.

In order to explain how contravariant type parameters are used, let's take a look at the following example. The example defines an abstract (MustInherit in Visual Basic) Shape class with an Area property. It also defines a ShapeAreaComparer class that implements IComparer<Shape> (IComparer(Of Shape) in Visual Basic). The implementation of the IComparer<T>.Compare method is based on the value of the Area property, so ShapeAreaComparer can be used to sort Shape objects by area.

You can also observe how the Circle class inherits Shape and overrides Area. The example creates a SortedSet<T> of Circle objects, using a constructor that takes an IComparer<Circle> (IComparer(Of Circle) in Visual Basic). However, instead of passing an IComparer<Circle>, the example passes a ShapeAreaComparer object, which implements IComparer<Shape>. The example can pass a comparer of a less derived type (Shape) when the code calls for a comparer of a more derived type (Circle), because the type parameter of the IComparer<T> generic interface is contravariant.

At the same time, the parameter type of the method (Shape) is less derived than the type that is being passed (Circle), so the call is type safe. Contravariance enable ShapeAreaComparer to sort a collection of any single type, as well as a mixed collection of types, that derive from Shape:[8]

```
using System;
using System.Collections.Generic;
abstract class Shape
{
    public virtual double Area { get {
return 0; }}
}
class Circle : Shape
{
    private double r;
    public Circle(double radius) { r =
radius; }
    public double Radius { get { return r;
}}
    public override double Area { get {
return Math.PI * r * r; }}
}
class ShapeAreaComparer : System.
Collections.Generic.IComparer<Shape>
{
    int IComparer<Shape>.Compare(Shape a,
Shape b)
    {
        if (a == null) return b == null ?
0 : -1;
```

[8] https://csjlsolutions.wordpress.com/tag/generic-type/, Wordpress

```
        return b == null?  1 : a.Area.
CompareTo(b.Area);
    }
}
class Program
{
    static void Main()
    {
        // You can pass ShapeAreaComparer,
which implements IComparer<Shape>,
        // even though the constructor for
SortedSet<Circle> expects
        // IComparer<Circle>, because type
parameter T of IComparer<T> is
        // contravariant.
SortedSet<Circle> circlesByArea =
            new SortedSet<Circle>(new
ShapeAreaComparer())
                { new Circle(7.2), new
Circle(100), null, new Circle(.01) };
        foreach (Circle c in circlesByArea)
        {
Console.WriteLine(c == null?  "null" :
"Circle with area " + c.Area);
        }
    }
}
/* This code example produces the following
output:
null
Circle with area 0.00031458979
Circle with area 162.8613162095
Circle with area 31415.92653
 */
```

CHAPTER 7

Functional Programming and Lambdas in C#

IN THIS CHAPTER

➤ Functional Programming

➤ Lambda Expression

➤ LINQ

We have covered Generics and its methods in the previous chapter, and now we are going to discuss Functional Programming. Functional Programming and its very concepts are becoming more critical to the software industry and data-driven applications. But to benefit from

DOI: 10.1201/9781003214779-7

functional programming, we don't have to use a strictly functional language like Haskell.

C# lets higher order functions through delegation. That means we can accept functions as parameters or return functions. In other words, functions are a first-class citizen in C#, which means we can structure together with a program in a functional manner just like functional languages,

Functional programming is older than computers. It came basically from mathematical logic (lambda calculus). In functional programming, we program with functions, and they don't change or mutate anything. They map an input to output.

FUNCTIONAL PROGRAMMING

Functional programming is a kind of programming paradigm in which one developer tries to bind everything in pure mathematical functions style. After a programmer manages to build the function and sends the function to the computer, it's the computer's turn to do its job. In general, the role of the computer is to evaluate the expression in the function and return the result. We can imagine that the computer acts as a calculator since it will analyze the expression from the function and yield the result to the user in a printed format. The calculator will evaluate a function composed of variables passed as parameters and expressions that form the body of the function. Their values substitute variables in the expression. We can give simple expressions and compound expressions using algebraic operators. Since expressions without assignments never alter the value, sub expressions need to be evaluated only once.

Suppose we have the expression 3 + 5 inside a function. The computer will return 8 as the result right after it thoroughly evaluates it. However, this is just a simple example of how the computer acts in evaluating an expression. A programmer can increase the computer's ability by creating a complex definition and expression inside the function. Not only can the computer evaluate the simple expression, but it can also evaluate the complex calculation, and expression is a declarative type of programming style. Its primary focus is how to solve instead of an imperative style where the exact direction is how to solve it. It uses expression instead of statements. An expression is evaluated to create a value, whereas a statement is executed to assign variables.

Benefits of Functional Programming[1]

- Pure functions make it simpler to reason about our code.

One of the most significant things that help us understand a piece of code better is to know where the source of change is. It is imperative because if we know for sure what a piece of code does and doesn't do, then we can alter our code with more conviction. Another benefit that this sort of code clarity can bring is when we need to find a problem in a system or debug.

- Testing pure functions are easier.

---

[1] https://hamidmosalla.com/2019/04/25/functional-programming-in-c-sharp-a-brief-guide/, Blog

There will be no hidden state or any dependency on the outside world in pure functions. This fact will make testing much easier because we don't have to worry about Mocking dependency or other hacks to prepare the functionality for a test.

• Debugging is smoother in programs written in functional style.

Writing pure functions that makes a program more obvious also can help with debugging. If we are aware with certainty what a function does, then all we have to do is to see what parameter was passed in and follow that value to see what went wrong.

• The declarative approach makes it easier to understand the code.

In object-oriented style of programming, we have statements that straightly alter and manipulate the values. This style of programming is known as imperative programming. But there is another style which is called declarative programming. In this kind of style, instead of changing the program directly, we write small pieces of functionality that do a specific thing and do it every well. In a way that it can be used with separate values, and we make up these functions together. As a result, we just announce what is required to be done instead of directly accumulate all the required calculations in one place. This eventually leads to a more readable code and can allow us to concentrate on solving the actual business problem.

- Method signature honesty.

This concept means that method signature of pure functions is thoughtful. Often in nonfunctional codes, we will encounter methods with no return value or parameter that does something. By viewing the signature, we don't know what the input and output of this function are and what it does. Also, the name of the methods is not an authentic source of information in this regard. So the only choice we have is to read the entire function.

But in pure functions, we immediately receive a lot of information about what a function does just by looking at its signature. Sometimes that is all we need to know about a function, and that's far more clear and faster than the nonpure functions.

Functional programming is a kind of programming paradigm in C# that is always combined with object-oriented programming. C# allows you to use imperative programming using object-oriented concepts, but it also uses declarative programming.[2] In declarative programming, you are using a more descriptive way to define what you need to do and not how you need to do some action, as we discussed earlier. For example, imagine that you want to find the top 10 books with a price less than 20 ordered by title. In functional programming, you can able to define something like:

```
books.Where(price<20).OrderBy(title).
Take(10);
```

[2] Jovan Popovic (2012), Code Project, Functional Programming in C#

Here, you just specify that you need to select books where the price is less than 40, order them by title, and take the first twenty. As you can see, you do not specify how this has to be done – only what you need to do.

The fundamental concept in functional programming is functions. In functional programming, we have to create functions as any other objects, manipulate them, pass them to other functions, etc. Therefore, we require more freedom as functions are not just parts of classes – they should be independent objects. In C#, you can use a function object as any other object type.

Function Types

Function objects must have some type. In C#, we can define either generic functions or strongly typed delegates. Delegates might be acknowledged as a definition of function prototypes where the method signature is defined. "Instance objects" of delegate types are pointers to functions (static methods, class methods) with a prototype that matches the delegate definition. An example of a delegate definition is shown in the following code:

```
delegate double MyFunction(double x);
```

This delegate defines a prototype of a function that has a double argument and returns the result as a double value. Note that only types are significant; actual names of methods and their arguments are arbitrary. This delegate type matches several trigonometric functions, exponential, polynomial, logarithm, and other functions. For example, you can simply define a function variable that references some math function, executes it via a function variable, and place the result in some other variable. An example is shown in the following listing:[3]

```
MyFunction f = Math.Sin;
double y = f(4); //y=sin(4)
f = Math.Exp;
y = f(4);
//y=exp(4)
```

Instead of firmly typed delegates, you can definitely use generic function types Func<T1, T2, T3, ..., Tn, Tresult> where T1, T2, T3, ..., Tn are types of the arguments (used if the function has some arguments), and Result is the return type. An example equivalent to the previous code is shown in the following listing:

```
Func<double, double> f = Math.Sin;
double y = f(4); //y=sin(4)
f = Math.Exp;
y = f(4);
//y=exp(4)
```

You can either define your named delegates or use generic types. Besides Func, you have two similar generic types:

- Predicate<T1, T2, T3, ...,Tn> that represents a function that returns a true/false value – equivalent to Func<T1, T2, T3, ...,Tn, bool>

- Action<T1, T2, T3, ...,Tn> that represents a procedure that does not return any value – equivalent to Func<T1, T2, T3, ...,Tn, void>

---

[3] https://hownot2code.com/2016/12/14/functional-programming-in-csharp/, hownot2code

The predicate is a function that takes some arguments and returns either a true or false value. In the following example, a predicate function that receives a string parameter is shown. The value of this function is set to String. IsNullOrEmpty. This function accepts a string argument and returns information whether or not this string is null or empty – therefore, it matches the Predicate<string> type:

```
Predicate<string> isEmptyString = String.
IsNullOrEmpty;
if (isEmptyString("Test"))
{
    throw new Exception("'Test' cannot be
empty");
}
```

Actions could be defined as procedures that can be executed. They accept some arguments yet return nothing. In the following example, one action that accepts string argument is shown, and it points to the standard Console. WriteLine method:

```
Action<string> println = Console.WriteLine;
println("Test");
```

When an action reference is called with the parameter, the call is forwarded to the Console.WriteLine method. When you use Action types, you just need to define the list of input parameters because there is no result. In this example, Action<string> is equivalent to Func<string, void>.

Once you define function objects, you can assign them other existing functions as shown in the previous listings or other function variables. Also, you can pass them to other functions as standard variables. If you want to assign a value to a function, you have the following possibilities:

- Point the function object to reference some existing method by name.

- Create an anonymous function using the lambda expression or delegate and assign it to the function object.

- Create a function expression where you are able to add or subtract a function and assign that kind of multicast delegate to the function object

Some examples of assigning values to functions are elaborated in the following listing:

```
Func<double, double> f1 = Math.Sin;
Func<double, double> f2 = Math.Exp;
double y = f1(4) + f2(5); //y=sin(3) +
exp(5)
f2 = f1;
y = f2(9);                   //y=sin(9)
```

In this case, methods are referred to as ClassName. MethodName. Instead of existing functions, you can dynamically create functions and assign them to variables. In this case, you can use either anonymous delegates or lambda expressions. An example is shown in the following listing:

```
Func<double, double> f = delegate(double
x) { return 3*x+1; }
double y = f(4); //y=13
```

```
f = x => 3*x+1;
y = f(5);
//y=16
```

In this code, we have allocated a delegate that accepts a double argument x and returns a double value 3*x+1. As this dynamically created function matches, Func<double, double>, it can be allocated to the function variable. In the third line, an equivalent lambda expression is allocated. As you can see, the lambda expression is identical to the function: it is just a function representation in the format parameters => return-expression. In the following table, some lambda expressions and equivalent delegates are shown:[4]

Lambda expression	Delegate
() => 3	delegate(){ return 3; }
() => DateTime.Now	delegate(){ return DateTime.Now; };
(x) => x+1	delegate(int x){ return x+1; }
x => Math.Log(x+1)-1	delegate(int x){ return Math.Log(x+1)-1; }
(x, y) => x+y	delegate(int x, int y){ return x+y;}
(x, y) => x+y	delegate(string x, string y){ return x+y;}

Lambda expression must have part for definition of argument names – if lambda expression does not have parameters, empty brackets () should be placed. If there is only one parameter in the list, brackets are not needed. After => sign, you need to put an expression that will be returned.

---

[4] https://hownot2code.com/2016/12/14/functional-programming-in-csharp/, hownot2code

The ability to build your own functions might be useful when you have to create your own new functions. For example, you can create some math functions that are not part of Math class, but you have to use them. Some of these functions are

```
asinh(x) = log(x + sqrt(x2 + 1))
acosh(x) = log(x + sqrt(x2 - 1))
atanh(x) = (log(1+x) - log(1-x))/2
```

Function Arithmetic

You can also add or subtract functions (delegates) in expressions. If you add two function values, when the resulting function variable is called, both functions will be implemented. This is the so called multicast delegate. You can also remove some functions from the multicast delegate. In the following example, we have added two functions that match the Action<string> type:[5]

```
static void Hello(string s)
{
System.Console.WriteLine("
Hello, {0}!", s);
}
static void Goodbye(string s)
{
System.Console.WriteLine("
Goodbye, {0}!", s);
}
```

---

[5] https://www.codeproject.com/Articles/375166/Functional-programming-in-Csharp, Codeproject

These methods accept a string parameter and return nothing. In the following code, how you can apply delegate arithmetic in order to manipulate multicast delegates is demonstrated:

```
Action<string> action = Console.WriteLine;
Action<string> hello = Hello;
Action<string> goodbye = Goodbye;
action += Hello;
action += (x) => { Console.WriteLine("
Greating {0} from lambda expression", x); };
action("First");  // called WriteLine,
Hello, and lambda expression

action -= hello;
action("Second"); // called WriteLine, and
lambda expression

action = Console.WriteLine + goodbye
        + delegate(string x){

Console.WriteLine("  Greating {0} from
delegate", x);
            };
action("Third");  // called WriteLine,
Goodbye, and delegate

(action - Goodbye)("Fourth"); // called
WriteLine and delegate
```

First, we have created three delegates pointing to the functions, WriteLine, Hello, and Goodbye. Then, we have added a function Hello and a new lambda expression to the first delegate. Operator += is used for attaching new functions that will be called by the multicast delegate. In the end, it will create a multicast delegate that will call all three functions once it is called. In the end, you see how you can create an expression and implement it. In the last statement, the result of the expression action – goodbye is a function mix in action without the Goodbye function.

C# Functional Programming

Now, we can move on to some functional programming examples. The fact that functions can be passed as arguments enables us to develop very generic constructions. As an example, imagine that you want to create a generic function that determines the number of objects in some array that satisfies some conditions. The following example shows how this function can be implemented:[6]

```csharp
public static int Count<T>(T[] arr,
Predicate<T> condition)
{
    int counter = 0;
    for (int i = 0; i < arr.Length; i++)
        if (condition(arr[i]))

counter++;
    return counter;
}
```

In this function, we are counting the elements in the array that satisfies the condition. Code that determines whether the condition is satisfied is not hard-coded in the function, and it is passed as an argument (predicate). This function

---

[6] https://www.codeproject.com/Articles/375166/Functional-programming-in-Csharp, Codeproject

can be used in various cases, such as counting the number of books where the title is longer than ten characters, or where the price is less than twenty, or counting the negative numbers in the array.

In addition, you can also use functional programming to replace some standard C# constructions. One typical example is using the block shown in the following listing:

```
using (obj)
{
obj.DoAction();
}
```

Using block is applied on the disposable objects. In the using block, you can operate with the object, call some of the methods, etc. When using block ends, the object will be simply removed. Or instead of using block, you can create your own function that will warp the action that will be applied to the object:

```
public static void Use<T>(this T obj,
Action<T> action) where T : IDisposable
{
        using (obj)
        {
action(obj);
        }
}
```

Higher-Order Functions

Using functions as regular objects allows us to apply them as arguments and results of other functions. Functions that manage other functions are called higher order functions.

Higher-order functions are common when using the LINQ library. As an example, if you want to convert a sequence to a new sequence using some function, you will use something like the Select LINQ function:

```
// Apply a function f T1 -> T2 to each
element of data using a List
public static IEnumerable<T2> MySelect<T1,
T2>(this IEnumerable<T1> data, Func<T1,
T2> f)
{
    List<T2> retVal= new List<T2>();
    foreach (T1 x in data) retVal.
Add(f(x));
    return retVal;
}
```

In this example, the function iterates through the list, applies the function f to each element, puts the result in the new list, and returns the collection. By modifying function f, you can create various transformations of the original sequence using the same generic higher order function.

Asynchronous Functions

One of the essential features of functions is that they can be called asynchronously, meaning you can start a function, continue with the work, and then wait until the function ends when you need results. Each function object in C# has the following methods:

- **BeginInvoke** that starts function execution but does not wait for the function to finish.

- **IsCompleted** that checks whether the execution is finished.

- **EndInvoke** that blocks execution of the current thread until the function is completed.

An example of asynchronous execution of the function:[7]

```
Func<int, int, int> f = Klass.SlowFunction;
//Start execution
IAsyncResult async = f.BeginInvoke(5, 3,
null, null); //calls function with
arguments (5,3)
//Check is function completed
if(async.IsCompleted) {
    int result = f.EndInvoke(async);
}
//Finally - demand result
int sum = f.EndInvoke(async);
```

In this example, a reference to some slow function that calculates the sum of two numbers is provided with the variable f. Alternatively, you can separately start invocation and pass arguments, check if the calculation was finished, and explicitly ask for the result. An example of that kind of function is shown in the following listing:

```
public class Klass{
     public static int SlowFunction(int x,
int y){
```

---

[7] https://www.codeproject.com/Articles/375166/Functional-programming-in-Csharp, Codeproject

```
Thread.Sleep(10000);

return x+y;
      }
}
```

Asynchronous Functions with Callbacks

In the previous example, you reviewed that arguments are passed to the function, but there are also additional parameters set to null. These arguments are:

- Callback function that will be called when the function finishes.

- Some objects that will be passed to the callback function.

This way, you do not need to explicitly check if the function was executed – just pass the callback function that will be called when the function finishes execution. An example of the call with callback is shown in the following code:[8]

```
Func<int, int, int> f = Klass.SlowFunction;
//Start execution
f.BeginInvoke(5, 3, async =>
                          {
                                     string
arguments = (string)async.AsyncState;
                                     var ar =
(AsyncResult)async;
                                     var fn =
(Func<int, int, int>)ar.AsyncDelegate;
```

---

[8] https://hownot2code.com/2016/12/14/functional-programming-in-csharp/, hownot2code

```
                                    int result
= fn.EndInvoke(async);

Console.WriteLine("f({0}) = {1}",
arguments, result);
                                    },
"5,3"
);
```

The callback function (or lambda expression in this example) takes a parameter async that has information about the asynchronous call. And when you cast the parameter of the lambda expression to AsyncResults, you can find the original function and call its EndInvoke method. As a result, you can print it on the console window.

Moreover, there is no need to explicitly check in the main code if the function has finished – just let it know what should be done when it is completed.

Tuples

Tuples are great way to dynamically form a required data structure. You can create tuples by passing a set of fields that belong to the tuple to the Tuple. An illustration of a function that uses tuples is shown below:

```
Random rnd = new Random();
Tuple<double, double> CreateRandomPoint()
{
    var x = rnd.NextDouble() * 10;
    var y = rnd.NextDouble() * 10;
    return Tuple.Create(x, y);
}
```

This function creates a random 2D point within area 10x10.

Tuples can also be used when you want to set generic functions that use structured data. If you want to create a predicate that determines whether a 2D point is placed within a circle with radius 1, you will use something like the following code:

```
Predicate<Tuple<double, double>> isInCircle;
isInCircle = t => (t.Item1*t.Item1+t.
Item2*t.Item2 < 1 );
```

Here, you have a function that takes a tuple with two double items and decides whether the coordinates are in the circle. You can access any field in the tuple using properties Item1, Item2, etc.

Tuples can also be applied when you want to create a data structure without creating a predefined class. Tuples can be used in the same code where you are using dynamic or anonymous objects, but one advantage of tuples is that you can use them as parameters or return values.

Now, let's review more complex example – suppose you have represented information about company as tuples of type Tuple<int, string, bool, int> where the first item is ID, second is the name of the company, third is a flag that marks the tuple as branch, and the last item is the ID of the head office. This is very common if you create some kind of query like SELECT id, name, isOffice, parentOfficeID and where you put each column in a separate dimension of the tuple. Now, we will create a function that takes a tuple and creates a new branch office tuple:[9]

---

[9] https://hownot2code.com/2016/12/14/functional-programming-in-csharp/, hownot2code

```
Tuple<int, string, bool, int?>
CreateBranchOffice(Tuple<int, string, bool,
int?> company){
    var branch = Tuple.Create(1, company.
Item2, company.Item3, null);
   Console.WriteLine(company);
    branch = Tuple.Create(10*company.
Item1+1, company.Item2 +
                        " Office", true,
company.Item1);
    Console.WriteLine(t);
    var office = new { ID = branch.Item1,
Name = branch.Item2,
IsOffice = branch.Item3,
ParentID = company.Item4 };
    return branch;
}
```

In this example, the function agrees on the company and creates a branch office. Both company and branch offices are represented as tuples with four items. Also, in this code, an anonymous object office with properties ID, Name, IsOffice, and ParentID is added, which is equivalent to tuple (this object is just created but not used anywhere). In this statement, you can see how easy it is to convert tuples to actual objects. The office object is an anonymous object; its class is not known by name outside of the function body. Therefore, you cannot define the return type of the function. If you want to return some dynamic structure instead of tuple, you would have to start a separate class instead of an anonymous class, or you will need to set the return type as dynamic, but in that case, you will lose information about the structure of the returned object.

Closures

When we are discussing functions, we should talk about the scope of variables. In the standard functions, we have the following types of variables:[10]

- Arguments that are passed to the function.

- Local variables that are defined and used inside the function body. They are smashed straightaway when function finishes.

- Global variables that are defined out of the function and referenced in the function body. These variables live even when the function ends.

If you need to develop a delegate or lambda expression, you should use arguments and local variables, and reference them outside the delegate. Example is shown in the following listing:

```
int val = 0;
Func<int, int> add = delegate(int delta) {
val+=delta; return val; };
val = 10;
var x = add(5);
// val = 15, x = 15
var y = add(7);
// val = 22, y = 22
```

Here, we have developed one delegate that adds the value of the parameter to the variable val that is defined outside the delegate.

---

[10] https://www.codeproject.com/Articles/375166/Functional-programming-in-Csharp, Codeproject

Now, what will be the result if variable val is a local variable in the higher-order function that returns this delegate? An example of that kind of function is shown here:

```
static Func<int, int> ReturnClosureFunction()
{
    int val = 0;
    Func<int, int> add = delegate(int
delta) { val += delta; return val; };
    val = 10;
    return add;
}
```

And with the calling code:

```
Func<int, int> add = ReturnClosureFunction();
var x = add(5);
var y = add(7);
```

This might be an issue because local variable val dies when ReturnClosureFunction is finished, but the delegate is returned and still lives in the calling code. If the delegate references the outside variable, it will be bound to the delegate as long as it lives in any scope. This means that the calling code above will set the values 15 in the variable x and 22 in the variable y. If a delegate references some variable outside his scope, this variable will act as a property of the function object and become a part of the function whenever the function is called.

LAMBDA EXPRESSION

The term "Lambda expression" has derived from "lambda" calculus which in turn is a mathematical term for defining functions. Here is an example of a lambda expression –

```
y ⇒ y * y
```

The above expression sets a parameter named y, and that value of y is squared. However, it is not possible to execute a lambda expression in this form. An example of a lambda expression in C# is shown below:[11]

```
using System;
using System.Collections.Generic;
using System.Linq;
using System.Text;

namespace lambdaexample {
    class Program {

        delegate int del(int i);
        static void Main(string[] args) {

            del myDelegate = y ⇒ y * y;
            int j = myDelegate(5);

Console.WriteLine(j);

Console.ReadLine();
        }
    }
}
VB
Module Module1
    Private Delegate Function del(ByVal i
As Integer) As Integer
```

[11] https://www.tutorialspoint.com/linq/linq_lambda_expressions.htm, Tutorialspoint

```
   Sub Main(ByVal args As String())

      Dim myDelegate As del = Function(y)
y * y
      Dim j As Integer = myDelegate(5)

Console.WriteLine(j)
Console.ReadLine()
End Module
```

Once the above code of C# or VB is compiled and executed, it produces the following result:

25

Async Lambdas

The lambda expression created by combining asynchronous processing with the async keyword is known as async lambdas. Below is an example of async lambda:

```
Func<Task<string>> getWordAsync = async()⇒
"hello";
```

A lambda expression within a query operator is examined by the same upon demand. It continually operated on each of the components in the input sequence and not the whole sequence. In the below example, the developer has used the "Where" operator to reclaim the odd values from the given list by using a lambda expression:[12]

---

[12] https://www.tutorialspoint.com/linq/linq_lambda_expressions.htm, Tutorialspoint

```csharp
//Get the average of the odd Fibonacci
numbers in the series...
using System;
using System.Collections.Generic;
using System.Linq;
using System.Text;

namespace lambdaexample {
    class Program {
        static void Main(string[] args) {

            int[] fibNum = { 1, 1, 2, 3, 5,
8, 13, 21, 34 };
            double averageValue = fibNum.
Where(num ⇒ num % 2 == 1).Average();

Console.WriteLine(averageValue);

Console.ReadLine();
        }
    }
}
```

```vb
VB
Module Module1

    Sub Main()

        Dim fibNum As Integer() = {1, 1, 2,
3, 5, 8, 13, 21, 34}
        Dim averageValue As Double = fibNum.
Where(Function(num) num Mod 2 = 1).Average()

Console.WriteLine(averageValue)
    Console.ReadLine()
    End Module
```

When the above code is executed, it shall deliver the following result –

- 7.33333333333333

In C#, type inference is used in different situations and that too without specifying the types explicitly. However, in a lambda expression, type inference will work only when each type has been specified as the compiler must be satisfied. Let's consider the following example:

```
delegate int Transformer (int i);
```

Here, the compiler uses the type inference to draw upon the fact that x is an integer, and this is done by calling the parameter type of the Transformer.

Variable Scope in Lambda Expression

There are certain rules applied for using the variable scope in a lambda expression, like variables that are initiated within a lambda expression are not meant to be visible in an outer method. There is also a rule that a captured variable is not to be removed unless the delegate referencing the same becomes eligible for removal too. Moreover, there is a rule that prohibits a return statement within a lambda expression to cause the return of an enclosing method. Here is an example to demonstrate variable scope in the lambda expression:[13]

---

[13] https://www.tutorialspoint.com/linq/linq_lambda_expressions.htm, Tutorialspoint

```csharp
using System;
using System.Collections.Generic;
using System.Linq;
using System.Text;

namespace lambdaexample {
   class Program {
      delegate bool D();
      delegate bool D2(int i);

      class Test {
         D del;
         D2 del2;

         public void TestMethod(int
input) {
            int j = 0;
            // Initialize the delegates
with lambda expressions.
            // Note access to 2 outer
variables.
            // del will be invoked within
this method.
            del = () ⇒ { j = 10; return j
> input; };

            // del2 will be invoked after
TestMethod goes out of scope.
            del2 = (x) ⇒ { return x == j;
};

            // Demonstrate value of j:
            // The delegate has not been
invoked yet.
```

```
Console.WriteLine("j = {0}", j);          //
Invoke the delegate.
          bool boolResult = del();

Console.WriteLine("j = {0}. b = {1}", j,
boolResult);
          }
        static void Main() {
           Test test = new Test();

test.TestMethod(5);
           // Prove that del2 still has a
copy of
           // local variable j from
TestMethod.
           bool result = test.del2(10);

Console.WriteLine(result);
Console.ReadKey();
          }
       }
    }
}
```

Once the above code is compiled, it shows the following
result –

- j = 0

- j = 10. b = True

- True

Statement Lambda

There is also statement lambdas that hold two or three
statements but are not included in the construction of

expression trees. A return statement must be inserted in a statement lambda. Basic syntax of statement lambda is:[14]

```
(params) ⇒ {statements}
Example of a statement lambda
using System.Collections.Generic;
using System.Linq;
using System.Text;
using System.Linq.Expressions;
namespace lambdaexample {
    class Program {
        static void Main(string[] args) {
            int[] source = new[] { 3, 8, 4,
6, 1, 7, 9, 2, 4, 8 };

            foreach (int i in source.Where(x ⇒
              {

if (x <= 3)
return true;
else if (x >= 7)
return true;
return false;
                }
            ))

Console.WriteLine(i);
Console.ReadLine();
        }
    }
}
```

---

[14] https://www.tutorialspoint.com/linq/linq_lambda_expressions.htm, Tutorialspoint

When the above code is fully implemented, it produces the following result:

- 3

- 8

- 1

- 7

- 9

- 2

- 8

Lambdas are employed as arguments in LINQ queries based on methods and never allowed to have a place on the left side of operators like is or as just like anonymous methods.[15] Although Lambda expressions are many like anonymous methods, these are not at all restricted to be used as delegates only.

LINQ

Language-Integrated Query (LINQ) is the name for a set of technologies based on the integration of query capabilities directly into the C# language. LINQ provides a consistent query experience for objects (LINQ to Objects), relational databases (LINQ to SQL), and XML (LINQ to XML).

---

[15] LINQ Microsoft .NET, tutorialspoint, *LINQ-Lambda Expressions*

Advantages of LINQ Include the Following:[16]

- It gives syntax highlighting and IntelliSense as LINQ is incorporated into C# language. These characteristics make it easier to produce accurate queries and to find mistakes at design time.

- Because LINQ queries are integrated into the C# language, you can write code much faster than if you were writing old-style queries.

- The integration of queries into the C# language also makes it easy to step through your queries with the integrated debugger.

- The hierarchical feature of LINQ allows you to easily see the relationship between tables, thereby making it easy to compose queries that join multiple tables quickly.

- The unitive foundation of LINQ allows you to use a single LINQ syntax when querying multiple data sources. This will enable you to get up to speed on new technologies much more quickly.

- Because LINQ is extensible, you can use your knowledge of LINQ to make new types of data sources queriable.

- After creating or discovering a new LINQ provider, you can leverage your knowledge of LINQ to quickly understand how to write queries against these new data sources.

---

[16] https://exceptionnotfound.net/csharp-in-simple-terms-14-linq-basics/, Exceptionnotfound

- Because LINQ is composable, you can quickly join multiple data sources in a single query or a series of related queries.

- The transformational features of LINQ make it easy to convert data of one type into a second type. For instance, you can quickly transform SQL data into XML data using LINQ.

- LINQ extends the language by the addition of query expressions, which are similar to SQL statements. LINQ query expressions can be used to extract conveniently and process data from arrays, enumerable classes, XML documents, relational databases, and third-party data sources.

- Query expressions can be used to query and transform data from any LINQ-enabled data source.

As mentioned above, LINQ allows us to query and manipulate groups of objects in C#. It does this in two ways: a query syntax that looks a lot like SQL queries and an API syntax, which consists of a set of method calls. Here's an example of the query syntax:[17]

```
List<int> myNumbers = new List<int> { 1,
2, 3, 4, 5, 6, 7, 8 };
var evenNumbers = from x in myNumbers
where x % 2 == 0
select x; //Get all even numbers
foreach(var num in evenNumbers)
```

---

[17] https://exceptionnotfound.net/csharp-in-simple-terms-14-linq-basics/, Exceptionnotfound

```
{
Console.WriteLine(num.ToString());
}
```

This code block selects the even numbers from the number set and outputs them to the Console.

Here's that same query using the API syntax:

```
List<int> myNumbers = new List<int> { 1,
2, 3, 4, 5, 6, 7, 8 };
var evenNumbers = myNumbers.Where(x => x %
2 == 0);
foreach(var num in evenNumbers)
{
    Console.WriteLine(num.ToString());
}
```

The API syntax is more concise in most situations, but specific queries are simpler to write and more easily understood with the query syntax.

Namespace
LINQ operations can be found in the System.Linq namespace:[18]

```
using System.Linq;
```

A basic LINQ query has three parts:

- **A from and an in clause.** The variable after the from specifies a name for an iterator. And the in clause specifies the collection we are querying from.

---

[18] Mathew Jones (2020), enf, LINQ – C# in Simple Terms

- **A select clause.** The select keyword points at what parts of the object to select. This can contain the entire object or only specific properties.

Here's a slightly more complex query, using a custom class:[19]

```
public class User
{
    public string FirstName { get; set; }
    public string LastName { get; set; }
    public int BirthYear { get; set; }
}
var users = new List<User>()
{
    new User()
    {
FirstName = "Terrance",
        LastName = "Johnson",

BirthYear = 2005
    },
    new User()
    {

FirstName = "John",
        LastName = "Smith",

BirthYear = 1966
    },
    new User()
    {
```

[19] https://exceptionnotfound.net/csharp-in-simple-terms-14-linq-basics/, Exceptionnotfound

```
FirstName = "Eva",
        LastName = "Birch",

BirthYear = 2002
    }
};
//Get the full combined name for people
born in 1990 or later
var fullNames = from x in users
where x.BirthYear >= 1990
select new { x.FirstName, x.LastName };
```

This illustrates an example of a projection: we can use LINQ to select properties of types without selecting the entire instance, and the resulting collection consists of only the properties we decided, not the whole object.

Filtering

There are many ways to filter the results of a query, apart from using a where clause. For example, we may want only the first item returned. To do this we must use the => operator, which is the "goes to" operator, to define a condition which records must match in order to be selected:[20]

```
var first = users.First(); //First element
in the collection
//First element that matches a condition
var firstWithCondition = users.First(x =>
x.BirthYear > 2001);
```

---

[20] https://exceptionnotfound.net/csharp-in-simple-terms-14-linq-basics/, Exceptionnotfound

The First() method calls an exception if no items are found. We can have it instead return a default value by using FirstOrDefault() (for all C# classes, the default value will be null):

```
//First element in collection or default
value
var firstOrDefault = users.
FirstOrDefault();
//First element that matches a condition
OR default value
var firstOrDefaultWithCondition = users.
FirstOrDefault(x => x.BirthYear > 2005);
```

We can also get exactly one item using Single() or SingleOrDefault():

```
var singleUser = users.Single(x =>
x.FirstName == "John");
var singleUserOrDefault = users.
SingleOrDefault(x => x.LastName ==
"Johnson");
```

Both Single() and SingleOrDefault() will show an exception if more than one item matches the condition.

Distinct

LINQ can also return all distinct items in a collection similar to this one:

```
var indistinctNumbers = new List<int> {4,
2, 6, 4, 6, 1, 7, 2, 7};
var distinctNumbers = indistinctNumbers.
Distinct();
```

You can also order results from a LINQ query by their properties using the methods OrderBy() and ThenBy():[21]

```
///Same User class as earlier
List<User> users = SomeOtherClass.GetUsers();
var orderedUsers = users.OrderBy(x => x.Fi
rstName)
.ThenBy(x => x.LastName); //Alphabetical
order
 //by  first name
//then last name
```

Note that we cannot use ThenBy() without first having an OrderBy() call.

There are also descending-order versions of these methods:

```
var descendingOrderUsers
    = users.OrderByDescending(x =>
x.FirstName)
.ThenByDescending(x => x.LastName); //
Reverse alphabetical order by

//first name, then
//by last name
```

We can also use the orderby and descending keywords in the query syntax:

```
var users = new List<User>();
var myUsers = from x in users
```

[21] https://exceptionnotfound.net/csharp-in-simple-terms-14-linq-basics/, Exceptionnotfound

```
orderby x.BirthYear descending, x.FirstName
descending
select x;
```

Aggregation

When managing a collection of number values, LINQ offers a few aggregation methods, such as Sum(), Min(), Max(), Count(), and Average(). Each of them can optionally be used after a Where() clause:

```
var numbers = new List<int> {1, 2, 3, 4,
5, 6, 7, 8, 9, 10};
Console.WriteLine("Sum: " + numbers.Sum());
//55
Console.WriteLine("Min: " + numbers.
Where(x=> x >= 2).Min()); //2
Console.WriteLine("Max: " + numbers.Where(x
=> x < 7).Max()); //6
//Returns the number of elements: 10
Console.WriteLine("Count: " + numbers.
Count());
//Returns the average of numbers whose
value is > 3. Result: 7
Console.WriteLine("Average: " + numbers.
Where(x => x > 3).Average());
```

Method Chaining

The great thing about LINQ's API syntax is that we can chain methods to produce concise, understandable code, even for complex queries.

For instance, let's say we have a collection of users, and we need to get all combined user names (first + last) ordered by the first name alphabetically, where the first letter of the

last name is J and the birth year is between 2000 and 2015.
The resulting LINQ method calls look like this:

```
var resultUsers = moreUsers.Where(x =>
x.LastName[0] == 'J'
                    && x.BirthYear >= 2000

&& x.BirthYear <= 2015)
                .OrderBy(x => x.FirstName)
                .Select(x => x.FirstName +
" " + x.LastName);
```

When using LINQ, the return type of a query is often of
type IEnumerable<T>. This is a generic interface that collections use to be enumerable, which means they can create
an iterator over the collection, which can return elements
within it.

However, sometimes what we really want is a full-blown
collection. For these times, LINQ includes methods that
will convert IEnumerable<T> to a concrete collection,
such as a List<T> or an array:

```
var numbers = new List<int> {1, 2, 3, 4,
5, 6, 7, 8, 9};
var evenNumbers = numbers.Where(x => x % 2
== 0);
List<int> list = evenNumbers.ToList();
int[] array = evenNumbers.ToArray();
```

Existence Operations

LINQ is also great to run checks for the existence of objects
in a collection that match given conditions. For example,

let's say we have a list of users, and we want to know if any of the users were born in the year 1997:[22]

```
bool isAnyoneBornIn1997 = users.Any(x =>
x.BirthYear == 1997);
```

We might also use Any() with no condition to check if there are any elements in a collection:

```
var users = SomeOtherClass.
GetCertainUsers();
bool hasAny = users.Any(); //True if there
are any elements, false otherwise.
```

We can also check if all the users in a particular collection were born in the year 1997:

```
bool isEveryoneBornIn1997 = users.All(x =>
x.BirthYear == 1997);
```

We can even check if a collection contains a particular value:

```
List<int> newNumbers = new List<int> {1,
2, 3, 4, 5, 6, 7, 8, 9};
bool hasAFive = newNumbers.Contains(5);
```

Additionally, LINQ allows us to perform the following set operations against two or more sets of objects:[23]

---

[22] https://exceptionnotfound.net/csharp-in-simple-terms-14-linq-basics/, Exceptionnotfound

[23] https://exceptionnotfound.net/csharp-in-simple-terms-14-linq-basics/, Exceptionnotfound

Intersection

An intersection is the group of objects that appear in both two lists:

```
var intersectionList1 = new List<int> {1,
2, 3, 4, 5, 6, 7, 8, 9};
var intersectionList2 = new List<int> {2,
4, 6, 8, 10, 12, 14};
var intersection = intersectionList1.
Intersect(intersectionList2);
//{2, 4, 6, 8}
```

Union

A union is the combined list of unique objects from two separate lists. An item which appears in both lists will only be listed in the union object once:

```
var unionList1 = new List<int> {5, 7, 3,
2, 9, 8};
var unionList2 = new List<int> {9, 4, 6,
1, 5};
var union = unionList1.Union(unionList2);
//{5, 7, 3, 2, 9, 8, 4, 6, 1}
```

Except

There is also the LINQ method Except(), which produces the elements that are in the first set, but not in the second set:

```
var exceptList1 = new List<int> {1, 2, 3,
4, 5, 6, 7, 8, 9};
var exceptList2 = new List<int> {7, 2, 8,
5, 0, 10, 3};
var except = exceptList1.
Except(exceptList2); //{ 1, 4, 6, 9}
```

Grouping

Imagine we have the following Book class:

```
public class Book
{
    public long ID { get; set; }
    public string Title { get; set; }
    public string AuthorName { get; set; }
    public int YearOfPublication { get;
set; }
}
```

Also, imagine that we have the following set of Book instances in a collection:

```
var books = new List<Book>()
{
    new Book()
    {
        ID = 1,
        Title = "Title 1",

AuthorName = "Author 1",
YearOfPublication = 2015
    },
    new Book()
    {
        ID = 2,
        Title = "Title 2",

AuthorName = "Author 2",
YearOfPublication = 2015
    },
    new Book()
```

```
    {
        ID = 3,
        Title = "Title 3",
AuthorName = "Author 1",
YearOfPublication = 2017
    },
    new Book()
    {
        ID = 4,
        Title = "Title 4",
AuthorName = "Author 3",
YearOfPublication = 1999
    },
    new Book()
    {
        ID = 5,
        Title = "Title 5",
AuthorName = "Author 4",
YearOfPublication = 2017
    },
};
```

One query we might want to run is this query using a group by query. A group by query has the following format:[24]

```
var results = from collectionVar in
collectionName
group collectionBar by collectionVar.
PropertyName
  into varGroupName
```

[24] https://exceptionnotfound.net/csharp-in-simple-terms-14-linq-basics/,
Exceptionnotfound

```
orderby varGroupName.Key //orderby is
optional
               select new {
                     Key = varGroupName.Key,
Objects = varGroupName.ToList()
                  };
```

Using this format, our query to get all books in order by publishing year looks like this:

```
List<Book> books = SomeOtherClass.
GetBooks();
var results = from b in books
group b by b.YearOfPublication into g
orderby g.Key
select new {Year = g.Key, Books =
g.ToList() };
```

We could then use a nested foreach loop to output all the books:

```
foreach(var result in results)
{
Console.WriteLine("Books published in " +
result.Year.ToString());

    var yearBooks = result.Books;
    foreach(var book in yearBooks)
    {
        Console.WriteLine(book.Title + " by "
+ book.AuthorName);
    }
}
```

CHAPTER 8

Dynamic Programming and Reflection

IN THIS CHAPTER

➢ What is Dynamic Programming

➢ Understanding Reflection

➢ Using the Dynamic Type

We have covered Functional Programming and Lambda in C# in the previous chapter, and now we will discuss Dynamic Programming and Reflection. Static languages

DOI: 10.1201/9781003214779-8

and dynamic languages are the two primary types of software development languages. The fundamental difference between a dynamic and a static language is how it operates its types or doesn't.

Static languages (statically typed languages) are spin around the very concept of statically typed variables. In dynamic languages, the variable Type doesn't have got to be defined straight away. In other words, variables are settled during "compile time" and in the dynamic in the "runtime" in the static language.

Then what does this mean?

In a static language, a variable is given its Type when the project is compiled, and it is positioned that way during the whole execution of the application. A variable can alter its Type several times in a dynamic language while the application is already running.

Below are the examples of static and dynamic languages:

- There are significant languages in both of these categories.

- There are significant languages in both of these categories.

Static	Dynamic
C	Javascript
Java	Perl
C#	Python
C++	PHP
F#	Ruby
Go	Objective-C

ADVANTAGES OF DYNAMIC
AND STATIC LANGUAGES

Dynamic languages, while being slower, are much simple to write.[1] And you can write them quickly without thinking about which Type to use or how to initialize them.

This comes at the price of identifying more bugs in runtime due to the interpreter missing to familiarize a variable's Type. At the same time, such code seems to be simple to read and is smaller overall, so the bugs generally have less space to hide in.

On the other hand, Static languages are generally considered quicker because they settle their types during the compilation phase. This helps enhance the application's performance and optimization.

Apart from fast, static languages are also being quick to fail. You can able to find bugs even before the application sets about as the compiler checks. This means only fewer bugs once the application is up and running.

Any language is significant in the right hands, and knowing any language to its core and utilizing its outstanding characteristics is the key to making great applications. Dynamic programming is an optimization approach that changes a complex problem into a sequence of more straightforward problems; its essential characteristic is the multistage nature of the optimization procedure. Dynamic programming gives a general framework for analyzing many problem types. Various optimization techniques can be adopted within this framework to sort out particular

---

[1] What is dynamic programming: introduction, Java T point

aspects of a more general formulation. Commonly, creativity is required before we can recognize that a specific problem can be cast effectively as a dynamic program. Often, subtle insights are necessary to restructure the formulation so that it can be solved effectively.

The definition of dynamic programming elaborates that it is a technique for sorting out a complex problem by breaking into a collection of simpler subproblems, solving each subproblem just once, and then storing their solutions to prevent recurring computations.

So now understand this approach by an example.

Contemplate an example of the Fibonacci series. We have provided you Fibonacci series below:

- 0, 1, 1, 2, 3, 5, 8, 13, 21, 34, 55, 89, 144, ...

We can simply understand that the numbers in the above series are not calculated anyway. Mathematically, we could simply write each of the terms that we have described using a formula:

- $F(n) = F(n-1) + F(n-2)$,

With the base values $F(0) = 0$, and $F(1) = 1$. To calculate the other numbers, we adhere to the above relationship.

An example for it is $F(2)$ is the sum $f(0)$ and $f(1)$, which is equal to 1.

So how could we calculate $F(20)$ here?

The $F(20)$ term here will be calculated using the nth formula of the Fibonacci series. The below figure elaborates that how $F(20)$ is calculated.

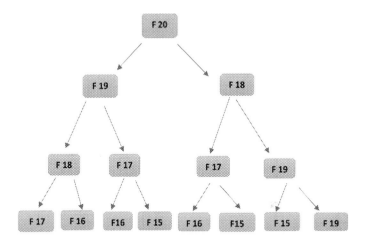

As we can get the idea in the above figure that F(20) is calculated as the sum of F(19) and F(18). In the dynamic programming approach, we attempt to divide the problem into somewhat like subproblems. We are adhering to this approach in the above case where F(20) into similar subproblems, i.e., F(19) and F(18). If we remind the definition of dynamic programming, it says the same subproblem must not be computed more except one. But, in the above case, the subproblem is calculated two times. In the example, F(18) is calculated twice; similarly, F(17) is also calculated twice. However, this technique is beneficial as it sorts out similar subproblems. Still, we need to be cautious while storing the results because we are not particular about keeping the result that we have computed once, then it can lead to wastage of resources.

The calculated results are saved in an array as a solution to the problem above. So startingly, we calculate F(16) and F(17) and keep their values in an array. The F(18) is calculated by summing the values of F(17) and F(16), which are saved in an array. The computed value of F(18) is protected in an array. The value of F(19) is calculated using the sum of F(18) and F(17), and their values are stored in an array. The computed value of F(19) is stored in an array. The value of F(20) can be calculated by adding the values of F(19) and F(18), and the values of both F(19) and F(18) are saved in an array. The final computed value of F(20) is saved in an array.

How does the dynamic programming approach work?

Below are the steps that the dynamic programming follows:

- It split the complex problem into simpler subproblems.

- It discovers the optimal solution to these subproblems.

- It stores the results of subproblems (memoization). The process of storing the results of subproblems that we get is called memorization.

- It reuses them so that the same subproblem is calculated more than once.

- Lastly, calculate the result of the complex problem.

The above five steps are the fundamental steps for dynamic programming. The dynamic programming is available for having properties such as:

Those problems that are having both overlapping subproblems and optimal substructures. Optimal substructure does mean that the solution of optimization problems can be acquired by simply clubbing the optimal solution of all the subproblems.

As in the case of dynamic programming, the space complexity would be as we store the intermediate results, but the time complexity would decrease.

Recursion vs. Dynamic Programming

Recursion risks to solve identical subproblems multiple times. This inefficiency is addressed and remedied by dynamic programming.

Recursion vs. Iteration

Concerning iteration, recursion has the following advantages and disadvantages:

- **Simplicity:** Often, a recursive algorithm is elegant and straightforward compared to an iterative algorithm

- **Space-inefficiency:** Every recursive call adds a layer to the system's call stack. If the number of stacked recursive calls gets too large, the result is a stack overflow.

Approaches of Dynamic Programming

There are two approaches to dynamic programming:

1. Top-down approach.

2. Bottom-up approach.

Top-Down Approach

The top-down approach adheres to the memorization technique, while the bottom-up approach adheres to the tabulation method. Here, memorization is the same as the sum of caching and recursion. Recursion is actually for calling the function, and caching is for storing the intermediate results.

Advantages

- It is elementary to get an idea and implement it.

- It resolves the subproblems only when it is needed.

- It is simple to debug.

Let's now recognize dynamic programming through an example.

```
int fib(int n)
{

if(n<0)

error;
 if(n==0)
 return 0;
 if(n==1)
return 1;
sum = fib(n-1) + fib(n-2);
}
```

In the abovementioned code, we have used the recursive approach to figure out the Fibonacci series. When the value of 'n' accentuates, the function calls will simultaneously increase, and computations will rise. In this case, the time complexity grows exponentially, and it becomes 2n.

One solution to this kind of issue is to use the dynamic programming approach. Rather than creating the recursive tree recurrently, we will be able to reuse the already calculated value. If we are trying to use the dynamic programming approach, the time complexity would be O(n).

When we give the dynamic programming approach in the implementation of the Fibonacci series, then the code would look like this:

```
static int count = 0;
int fib(int n)
{
if(memo[n] != NULL)
return memo[n];
count++;

if(n<0)

error;
 if(n==0)
 return 0;
 if(n==1)
return 1;
sum = fib(n-1) + fib(n-2);
memo[n] = um;
}
```

In the code we put forth, we used the memorization technique to store the results in an array to use the values again. This is also known as the top-down strategy, in which we start at the top and work our way down to the subproblems.

Bottom-Up Approach

The bottom-up approach is a kind of technique that can be used to implement dynamic programming. It utilizes the tabulation technique to implement the dynamic programming approach. It sorts out the same kind of problems, but it also eliminates the recursion. If we eliminate the recursion, there is no stack overflow issue and no overhead of the recursive functions. In this tabulation technique, we can resolve the problems and store the results in a matrix.

The bottom-up is the approach used to keep away from the recursion, thus saving the memory space. The bottom-up algorithm sets off from the beginning, whereas the recursive algorithm begins from the end and works backward. In the bottom-up approach, we set off from the base case to figure out the answer for the end as we are already familiar that the base cases in the Fibonacci series are 0 and 1. Since the bottom approach begins from the base cases, we will set off from 0 and 1.

Key Points

We solve all the smaller subproblems needed to solve the larger subproblems then move to the more significant problems using smaller subproblems.

We use for loop to the subproblems.

The tabulation or table filling method is another name for the bottom-up approach.

DYNAMIC PROGRAMMING IN C#

C# 4.0 introduces a flexible and declarative programming style using the dynamic language runtime (DLR) library.

This style is called dynamic programming.[2] Programmers can now use the "Dynamic" keyword (the new static Type) for creating typed objects or placeholders. These dynamic type objects bypass compile-time type checking. That's why the types of these placeholders are unknown until runtime. In .NET Framework 4.0 architecture, DLR is built on top of common language runtime (CLR) to support the dynamism of dynamic programming languages like Python and Ruby.

How to Use Dynamic

First, we have to show you some code snipped from a dynamic type declaration. You have got to declare a variable whose static Type is dynamic. As discussed above, the dynamic is typed objects or placeholders (like var in Visual Basic) that indicate to the compiler that object type will be resolved dynamically.

```
dynamic objdynamic = "Dynamic Programming
Sample";
dynamic objstring = objdynamic;
dynamic objint = 1;
dynamic objlist = new List<int> { 1, 2, 3 };
```

In the above example, the Type of "objstring" object will be System. String at runtime. You can also give a return value of any method to dynamic objects. The following code snippet illustrates:

```
static void Main ( string[] args )
{
```

---

[2] CodeGuru staff (2010), Dynamic programming using C# 4.0 and Microsoft visual studio, Codeguru

```
dynamic objdynamic = GetDynamicObject();
}
public static int GetDynamicObject ( )
{
int i = 3;
int j = 4;
return i+j;
}
```

Now let us show you few examples of RuntimeBinding-Exception that can happen while working with a dynamic static type.

```
dynamic dynullvalue = null;
dynamic objtype = dynullvalue.GetType ( );
```

The above code will work in compile time but will throw an exception in runtime as the second statement makes head-way to access the Type of null reference. Dynamic objects can't perform object binding on a null reference.

```
dynamic objdynamic = "Dynamic Programming
Sample";
int i = objdynamic;
```

The above code will give an implicit conversion error in runtime (string can't be converted to integer). Dynamic will also give runtime exceptions for nonexisting property or method. The following code snippet is going to throw RuntimeBindingException for the same reason.

```
dynamic objdynamic = "Dynamic Programming
Sample";
```

```
int i = objdynamic.Intvalue;    // Property
doesn't exists
int j = objdynamic.GetIntValue ( ); //
Method doesn't exists
```

Now let us illustrate to you a working example dynamic keyword. For creating the sample C# programming console application, I have used Microsoft Visual Studio 2010 Ultimate Edition with .NET Framework 4.0. First, I have created a currency conversion class with 1 method named ConvertCurrency(). This ConvertCurrency() method converts source currency to destination currency type using a conversion factor. The following is a code snippet of the CurrencyConvert class.

```
public class CurrencyConvertionService :
ICurrencyConvertionService
public double ConvertCurrency ( string
from currency, the string to currency,
double amount )
                {

if ( fromcurrency.Length <=0 || tocurrency.
Length <= 0 )

return 0;

if ( amount <=0 )
return 0;
switch ( from currency )
                {

case "INR":
```

```csharp
if ( tocurrency.Trim ( ).ToString ( ) ==
"USD" )
                          return amount *
0.0214938;

if ( tocurrency.Trim ( ).ToString ( ) ==
"EUR" )
                          return amount *
0.0175683;

if ( tocurrency.Trim ( ).ToString ( ) ==
"GBP" )
                          return amount *
0.0145759;
                  break;

case "USD":
                     if ( tocurrency.
Trim ( ).ToString ( ) == "INR" )
                          return amount *
45.67;
if ( tocurrency.Trim ( ).ToString ( ) ==
"EUR" )

                          return amount *
0.817748;

if ( tocurrency.Trim ( ).ToString ( ) ==
"GBP" )
                          return amount *
0.678214;
break;

case "GBP":
```

```
if ( tocurrency.Trim ( ) .ToString ( ) ==
"INR" )
                                return amount *
68.5929;

if ( tocurrency.Trim ( ) .ToString ( ) ==
"EUR" )

                        return amount *
1.20610;

if ( tocurrency.Trim ( ) .ToString ( ) ==
"USD" )
                                return amount *
1.47431;

break;
default:
return 0
}

return 0;
                }
            }
```

Next, we wrote the main() method to show how both static CurrencyConvert class and dynamic objects work. You will get an identical converted value for both cases if you are passing the same input parameters. The main () method code example is shown below:

```
class Program
            {
 static void Main ( string[] args )
```

```
                {

CurrencyConvert objConverter = GetConverter
( );

Console.WriteLine (
objConverter.ConvertCurrency ( "USD",
"INR", 50 ));

Console.Read ( );

// Dynamic

dynamic dyobjConverter = GetConverter ( );

Console.WriteLine ( dyobjConverter.
ConvertCurrency ( "USD", "INR", 50 ) );

Console.ReadLine ( );
                }

public static CurrencyConvert GetConverter ( )
                {

CurrencyConvert objConverter = new
CurrencyConvert ( );

return objConverter;
                }
            }
```

Dynamic and Overloading of Methods

In overloaded methods, the runtime determines which functions must be called based on the data type of the input argument. We developed a calculator class with two over-loaded versions of the add function to show the runtime resolution of dynamic objects. The following is a sample of code from my calculator class.

```
class Calculator
          {
public double Add ( int i, double j )
               {
return i+j;
               }
public double Add ( int i, int j )
               {
return System.Convert.ToDouble( i+j );
                }
```

Next, we have written the following code section in the main() method to call the add methods dynamically.

```
static void Main ( string[] args )
               {
Calculator objcal = new Calculator ( );
dynamic myDynamic =  GetIntValue ( );
dynamic myDynamic1 =
GetDoubleValue ( );
Console.WriteLine( objcal.Add ( myDynamic,
myDynamic1 ));
               Console.ReadLine ( );
dynamic myDynamic2 =  GetIntValue ( );
dynamic myDynamic3 =  GetIntValue ( );

Console.WriteLine ( objcal.Add (
myDynamic2, myDynamic3 ) );
```

```
Console.ReadLine ( );

                    }

public static int GetIntValue ( )
                    {

return 10;
                    }

public static double GetDoubleValue ( )
                    {

return 10.25;
                    }
```

The first time objcal.Add (myDynamic, myDynamic1) method invocation. Because the dynamic input parameter types are integer and double, the Add (int i, double j) overloaded method of the calculator class is called. Similarly, objcal invokes the Add function for the second time. Add (myDynamic2, myDynamic3), an overloaded method of the calculator class for the matching input parameters data type, is called by the Add (int I int j) expression.

Conclusion

Developers may now make interop calls using dynamics. You may also use dynamic to call the COM object's function. The dynamic keyword can be used to replace the sophisticated reflection code you've previously written, but it comes with certain drawbacks. We can't invoke extension methods or anonymous functions, for example.

UNDERSTANDING REFLECTION

Reflection is when managed code able to read its metadata to figure out assemblies. It allows code to inspect other code within the same System.Elaborate, Java's static typing system isn't designed to support the "doSomething" method if the object does not conform to a known interface. But with Reflection, your code can view the object and figure out if it has the "doSomething" method. In addition, you can call it if required.

With Reflection in C#, you can dynamically make an instance of a type and stitch that Type to an existing object. Moreover, you can get the Type from a current object and access its properties. Whenever you use attributes in your code, Reflection provides you access as it gives objects of Type that describe modules, types, and assemblies.

Defining Reflection in C#

To get an idea about Reflection, there are a few basics you should know about modules, types, and members:

- Assemblies include modules.
- Modules include types.
- Types include members.

You have to use Reflection when you need to check the contents of an assembly as you can get all members of the object by typing "." before an object when viewing your Visual Studio editor IntelliSense.

A program mirrors itself when it extracts metadata from its assemblies, then uses it to modify its behavior or inform the user. You can evaluate Reflection to C++RTTI (Runtime Type Information), except it has tremendous capabilities. When you write a C# program that wants to use Reflection, you can use the TypeOf operator or the GetType() method to get the object's Type.

A Simple Use Case

Reflection can also create applications called type browsers, allowing users to select types and then read the data provided. This example elaborates how to use the static method GetType to figure out the type of a variable:

```
// Using GetType to obtain type
information:
int i = 42;
System.Type type = i.GetType();
System.Console.WriteLine(type);
```

The above example will get following output:

- System.Int32
- Examples of Reflection in C#
- Implementing Reflection in C# needs a two-step process.
- First get the "type" object,
- Use the Type to browse members such as "properties" and "methods."

This is the way you have to create instances of the DateTime class from the system assembly:

```
// create instance of class DateTime
DateTime dateTime = (DateTime)Activator.
CreateInstance(typeof(DateTime));
```

To access the sample class Calculator from Test.dll assembly, the Calculator class must be defined as the following:

```
namespace Test
{
public class Calculator
{
        public Calculator() { ... }
        private double _number;
        public double Number { get { ... }
set { ... } }
        public void Clear() { ... }
        private void DoClear() { ... }
        public double Add(double number) {
... }
        public static double Pi { ... }
        public static double GetPi() { ...
}

}
}
```

Then, you will be able to use Reflection to load the Test.dll assembly:

```
// dynamically load an assembly from file
Test.dll
Assembly testAssembly = Assembly.
LoadFile(@"c:\Test.dll");
```

To make an instance of the calculator class:

```
// get type of class Calculator from just
loaded assembly
Type calcType = testAssembly.GetType("Test.
Calculator");
//create instance of class Calculator
object calcInstance = Activator.
CreateInstance(calcType);
```

And obtain its members (the following examples elaborate getting values for the public double Number property):

```
// get info about the property: public
double Number
PropertyInfo numberPropertyInfo = calcType.
GetProperty("Number");
//get value of property: public double Number
double value = (double)numberPropertyInfo.
GetValue(calcInstance, null);
//set value of property: public double Number
numberPropertyInfo.SetValue(calcInstance,
10.0, null);
```

How Reflection in C# Works

The critical class for Reflection is the System.Type class is an abstract class representing a type in the Common Type System (CTS).[3] Whenever you use this class, you can find the types used in a module and namespace and determine if a given type is a reference or value type. You can analyze the corresponding metadata tables to look through these items:

---

[3] Alexandra Altvater (2017), How C# work with code example, Stacky

- **Fields.**

- **Properties.**

- **Methods.**

- **Events.**

Late bindings can also be attained through Reflection. To elaborate, you are not able to the idea of which assembly to load during compile time. In this circumstance, you can ask the user to enter the assembly name and Type during the run time, so the application can load the appropriate assembly. With the System.Reflection.Assembly type, you can make available three static types that let you load an assembly directly:

1. LoadFrom.

2. LoadFrom.

3. LoadWithPartialName.

When you contemplate that an assembly is a logical DLL or EXE and a manifest is a comprehensive overview of an assembly, then it is the rationale that a portable executable (PE) file for CTS would have the extension of .dll or .exe. Within the PE file is mostly metadata, which includes a variety of multiple tables:

- Method definition table.

- Filed definition table.

- Type definition table.

When you analyze these tables, you can able to retrieve an assembly's attributes and types.

Uses for Reflection C#

There are a whole lot of uses of Reflection in C# as we here mentioned some:

- Use Module to acquire all global and non-global methods defined in the module.

- Use MethodInfo to look at parameters, name, return type, access modifiers, and implementation details.

- Use EventInfo to figure out the event-handler data type, the name, declaring Type, and custom attributes.

- Use PropertyInfo to get the declaring Type, reflected Type, data type, name, and writable status of a property or to get and set property values.

- Use CustomAttributeData to figure out information on custom attributes or to review attributes without creating more instances.

- Other uses for Reflection include constructing symbol tables to determine which fields to persist and through serialization.

- Use ConstructorInfo to get data on the parameters, access modifiers, and implementation details of a constructor.

- Use Assembly to load modules listed in the assembly manifest.

USING DYNAMIC TYPE

Dynamic data type was introduced with C# 4.0. Dynamic data types are dynamic and don't require initialization at the time of declaration. It also means that a dynamic type does not have a predefined type and can store any data.

How Does Dynamic Type Work?

Honestly, when you declare a variable dynamic, you instruct the compiler to shut off the compile-time type checks. Dynamic is System.Object type as secretive, but it doesn't require casting a value before using it explicitly. We will discuss it later.

For now, let's illustrate how dynamic Type works on some examples.

We can set off by creating a dynamic variable:

```
dynamic testVariable = 5;
Console.WriteLine(testVariable.GetType());
```

Can you imagine the output of the Console?Writeline()? It's not hard to imagine – it is, of course, System.Int32.

So what happens if we alter the value of the testVariable to something entirely different like "Hello World"?

Can we do that?

Let's see.

```
testVariable = "Hello World";
Console.WriteLine(testVariable.GetType());
Now we get the output System.String.
```

But if we would like to do something like incrementing a value now, we'll get an exception:

```
Console.WriteLine(testVariable++);
```

The code will compile, but we will get an exception when we run the application:

RuntimeBinderException is the exception you will see the most when you work with dynamic types. As the exception message, we cannot use the ++ operator on a variable of type string, as stated in the exception notice. So that means that the dynamic Type behaves like the last Type we've assigned to it.

One more example of wrapping it up.

We have a class that provides us the instance of some logger implementation:

```csharp
public class Logger
{
public void LogInfo(string message)
{
Console.WriteLine($"INFO: {message}");
}
public void LogWarning(string message)
{
Console.WriteLine($"WARNING: {message}")
}
public void LogError(string message)
{
Console.WriteLine($"ERROR: {message}")
}
}
public class LoggerFactory
{
public static Logger GetLogger()
{
        return new Logger()
}
```

```
}
dynamic logger = LoggerFactory.GetLogger();
logger.LogInfo("Hi");
logger.LogWarning("You are going to enter
a time warp");
logger.LogError("System is
malfunctioning");
logger.LogTrace("Communication lost");
```

When we consider compiler, everything is comfortable.[4] But once more, we get the RuntimeBinderException because LogTrace method is not expounded.

Short Overview of DLR

So now have understood how the dynamic type works, let's discuss what's behind the curtains a little.

DLR or Dynamic Language Runtime makes dynamic Type easy to use in a C#, statically typed language. DLR attaches a set of services to the CLR that do dynamic work.

As we can see, the services DLR included in the already existing functionalities of CLR include Call Site Caching, Expression Trees, and Dynamic Object Interoperability.

Call Ste Caching

DLR provides a way to cache previously called operations to achieve maximum efficiency in operation execution. A dynamic call site is where you may use the a.b() and a+b functions on dynamic objects. DLR caches the types of objects used while executing these operations and stores

[4] Vladimir Pecanac (2020), Advanced dynamic code type, code maze

them in a cache. If a similar operation is performed once more, DLR can retrieve the information from that cache.

Expression Trees

Expression trees constitute code in a tree-like data structure, where each node is an expression, for example, a method call or a binary operation. DLR has extended LINQ expression trees with assignment, control flow, and other language-modeling nodes.

Dynamic Object Interoperability

To earn operability with different languages and enable authors to implement dynamic libraries, DLR gives a set of classes and interfaces used for this purpose: IDynamicMetaObjectProvider, ExpandoObject DynamicMetaObject, and DynamicObject.

The advantages of DLR are:

- Simplified portability of dynamic languages to .NET.

- Allow dynamic features in static languages.

- Enhanced sharing of libraries and communication between static and dynamic languages.

- Fast dispatch and invocation (using caching).

In conclusion, DLR makes the dynamic type work as we know it, and we wouldn't be able to use dynamic Type without it and the mechanisms it renders.

Why Should We Use the Dynamic Type

By now, you might have a glimpse of where you can able to use a dynamic type. But let's wade through some common scenarios in which dynamics could potentially enhance our applications and ensure our lives as developers are a bit comfortable.

First of all, let's make it evident that dynamic is not a magical solution try. We shouldn't try to use it just because we can able to.

While it has its own merits, dynamic objects are harder to work with while writing code since we don't have an Intellisense for them due to the nature of dynamic Type. On the other hand, if we need to implement dynamic Type everywhere, we probably use the wrong Type of language. Dynamic languages are best suited for those kinds of cases.

So what are the typical cases to apply a dynamic type to:

- for Communicating with other kinds of dynamic languages
- Simplifying responses from API calls when we are unfamiliar with what type of object to expect (or we don't care)

Ok, so let's look into some concrete examples of dynamic in action.

Dynamic vs. Reflection

Reflection is a mechanism to acquire a type of abstract System.Object, and to invoke its members without any glimpse of the concrete Type of that object.

Take an example, let's see what a typical reflection flow looks like:

```
EmployeeFactory employeeFactory =
GetEmployeeFactory();
object firstEmployee = employeeFactory.
GetFirstEmployee();
Type firstEmployeeType = firstEmployee.
GetType();
object workStatusObject =
firstEmployeeType.
InvokeMember("GetWorkStatus", BindingFlags.
InvokeMethod, null, firstEmployee, null);
WorkStatus workStatus = Enum.Parse<WorkSta
tus>(workStatusObject.ToString());
Console.WriteLine(workStatus);
```

Although very complicated and extensive for its purpose, this piece of code retrieves an employee's work status. All of that code was written to call a single method.

Because our EmployeeFactory class returns a generic System as an employee, this is the case. Type of object. System. The object is the basic class for all other classes, and we may use it if we don't know what type of object we should anticipate.

To call the method of a System and for the object, we must first determine what type of object it is. We do that by calling the object.GetType() method. Then, using the InvokeMember() method, we'll be able to execute the GetWorkStatus function on the firstEmployee object.

We can finally determine the firstEmployee's work status after some enum parsing.

A bit complicated as it seems, but it works.

Now let's look into how the same example is like by using dynamic:

```
EmployeeFactory employeeFactory =
GetEmployeeFactory();
dynamic firstEmployee = employeeFactory.
GetFirstEmployee();
WorkStatus workStatus = firstEmployee.
GetWorkStatus();
Console.WriteLine(workStatus);
```

Well, that looks much easier and quite simple to read. Types and method names didn't have to be thought of as strings.

As a result of the dynamic vs. reflection struggle, we shall get:

- Cleaner and more readable code.

- Good performance due to dynamic Type caching.

- Not having hardcoded strings in our code.

- Simpler implementation.

This example is for just illustration purposes only. Both reflection and dynamic must be used sparingly and not just "because we can."

Both of them can reduce the performance of an application and introduce bugs we could have ousted by properly implementing static mechanisms and abstractions.

Var vs. Object vs. Dynamic
If you are a beginner to the C# world, you might still be discerning these three main keywords.

Let's discuss them below.

Var Keyword

Var is used to type a variable implicitly in a method scope. The variable is strongly typed, but the compiler makes up its mind which Type it will be in the runtime. We can even notice the Type by hovering over the var keyword.

```
var imNumber = 10; //implicitly typed variable
int exNumber = 10; //explicitly typed variable
```

Our opinion is that var enhances the readability of the code, and it should be used because, generally, we don't need to type our variables explicitly.

In times if the types are complicated.

Take an example, Dictionary<string, IEnumerable <Employee>> or something even more complicated. The Type of the variable is not able to alter at runtime.

Object Keyword

The object is an alias for System. An object is the base class in C#. Every class in C# is obtained from System.Object, and we can employ that fact to make a more generic codebase. We will get the concrete Type of the object we are working on within runtime through the object type. At the same time, we can earn pretty much anything in terms of abstraction with the System.Object, sometimes we are strained to use reflection to achieve our goal, which is not ideal.

If you want to use the type that is assigned to the System. Object variable, we need to profoundly cast it first. For example:

```
object testObj = 10;
testObj = (int)testObj + 10;
```

Dynamic Keyword

Dynamic is an object type, but it bypasses compiler type checks. We can give anything to a dynamic variable and not be perplexed about the compiler or the Type. It uses the power of DLR, which is an extension of CLR. Although bypassing compiler checks is simple, it could potentially lead to unexpected behavior if not used cautiously. We don't need to cast dynamics before trying out different operations explicitly.

```
dynamic testDynamic = 10;
testDynamic = testDynamic + 25;
RuntimeBinderException
```

RuntimeBinderException is the exception we could get at execution time if a dynamic type fails to sort out the operation we provided on a type that doesn't support it.

To make it simple terms, imagine you are trying to do something on a static type and that static Type doesn't implement that behavior.

Like trying to increment a string. Or calling.Split() on an integer.

It's not that easy, though, and there is some problem that we must be aware of. For example, calling the.Count() on a dynamic object that has been given ICollection:

```
public static void
ExamplePrintCount(ICollection collection)
{
dynamic d = collection;
Console.WriteLine("Static typing: {0}",
collection.Count);
```

```
Console.WriteLine("Dynamic typing: {0}",
d.Count);
}
```

If we operate this example by giving an int array:

```
ExamplePrintCount(new int[20]);
```

What do you imagine about the result?

Suppose you guessed that first Console.WriteLine() will output 2, and that we'll get RuntimeBinderException in the second one, you thought it is fitting.

Appraisal

C# is a modern object-oriented, general-purpose programming language, developed by Microsoft together with the. NET platform. There is extremely diverse software developed with C# and on the .NET platform: office and web applications, desktop applications, mobile applications, games, and many others. C# is a high-level language that resembles to Java and C++ and, to a certain extent, languages like Delphi, VB.NET, and C. Since all C# programs are object-oriented, they hold a set of definitions in classes that consist of methods and those methods contain the program logic—the directives which the computer runs.

It is without a doubt that C# is one of the most popular programming languages. It is used by millions of developers worldwide. Moreover, because C# is created by Microsoft as part of their new platform for development and execution of applications, the .NET Framework, the language is widely applied among Microsoft-based corporations, organizations, and individual developers.

C# is an object-oriented programming language; such are all modern programming languages used for building software systems. The advantages of object-oriented programming are brought up in many passages throughout

DOI: 10.1201/9781003214779-9

this book, but, as for now, you can think of object-oriented languages as languages that have properties and are able to perform actions. This book covers the concepts of object-oriented programming through a real-world example. Then you will dive into advanced-level concepts such as generics and collections and get acquainted with objects and LINQ. Toward the end, you will work with application components that illustrate all the concepts explained in this book.

This book takes a unique and practical approach to teach C# to absolute beginners. It begins by teaching you the basic fundamentals and gets you acquainted with C# programming by introducing important features and nuances of the language in a hands-on way, helping you grasp the concepts in a fluid manner.

We will start by examining primitive types and variables in C#—what they are and how to work with them. First, we will review all the data types—integer types, real floating-point types, Boolean, character types, strings, and object types. We will continue with variables, their characteristics, how to declare them, how they are assigned a value, and what variable initialization is. It is also important to familiarize oneself with the main categories of data types in C#—value and reference types. We shall also discuss literals, what they are and what kinds of literals there are.

After getting to know the basics of the language, you are expected to spend some time learning arrays as a means for operating sequence of elements of the same type. This book explains what they are and how we can declare, create, and instantiate arrays to provide access to their elements. You will be able to examine one-dimensional and multidimensional arrays and learn the various ways for iterating through an array, reading from the standard input and writing to the standard output. Many exercises as examples, which can be solved using arrays, will be provided along the way, just to show you how useful these tools can be.

In addition, you will get to know in detail the subroutines in programming, which are called methods in C#. We will describe when and why methods are used; show how methods are declared and what a method signature is. You will learn how to create a custom method and how to invoke it subsequently, using parameters and some established practices when dealing with methods. Again, all of this will be backed up with examples explained in details.

Going back to the principles of object-oriented programming, be prepared to look into notions of class inheritance, interfaces implementation, data and behavior abstraction, data encapsulation and hiding implementation details, polymorphism, and virtual methods. Not to mention the principles of cohesion and coupling. We will also briefly outline object-oriented modeling and object model creation based on a specific technical problem.

You will also be exposed to some of the more sophisticated capabilities of C#. To be more specific, we will pay special attention to clarifying how to make queries to collections using lambda expressions and LINQ. This book thoroughly explains how to add functionality to already created classes, using extension methods. We will familiarize ourselves with anonymous types and briefly describe their nature and usage. Moreover, we will also review lambda expressions and show in practice how most of the built-in lambda functions work.

This book also includes a section on the popular .NET technology Language Integrated Query (LINQ), which allows execution of various queries (such as searching, sorting, summation, and other group operations) on arrays, lists, and other objects. It is placed toward the end on purpose, after the essential chapters on data structures and algorithms complexity. The reason behind this is that the good programmer should know what happens when they sort a list or search in an array according to criteria and how many operations these actions take. If LINQ is applied, it is not obvious how a given query operates and how much time it takes. LINQ is a very powerful and widely used technology, but it has to be mastered at a later stage, after you are well familiar with the basics of programming, and the main algorithms. Otherwise, you risk learning how to write inefficient code without understanding how it works and how many operations it runs in the background.

As a beginner, there is no need to worry since it is pretty simple to learn C#. Yet to know C#, you should have at least a basic idea of writing code, even if you have yet to build your first application or program. The learning curve for C# is relatively low when compared to more complex languages.

In case you are looking to start a career in the industry, try checking out a website with job offers for programmers, and you will see for yourself that the demand for C# and .NET specialists is very high. The demand for PHP, C++, and other technology specialists is far lower than that for C# and Java engineers. At the same time, for good, experienced programmers, the language they use is of no significant meaning because they know how to program. Whatever language and technology they might require for the task, they will be able to master it quickly. Therefore, your goal is not only to learn C#, but rather to gain an understanding of programming. After you master the fundamentals of programming and learn to think algorithmically, when you acquaint with other programming languages, you will see for yourself how much in common they have with C# and how easy it will be to learn them.

Programming is built upon principles that almost never change over the years, and this book teaches you these very principles. You should realize that the essence of programming is to control the work of the computer on different levels. This is done with the help of "orders" and "commands" from the programmer, also known as programming instructions. To "program" means to coordinate the work of the computer through sequences of instructions. These commands are given in written form and are implicitly followed by the computer (respectively by the operating system, the CPU and the peripheral devices). Thus, to "program" means to be able to script multiple sequences of instructions in order to organize the work of the computer to achieve something as a result. These sequences of instructions are called "computer programs" or "scripts." A sequence of steps to achieve, complete some work, or get a certain result is called an algorithm. This is how programming is related to algorithms.

To put it simply, programming involves describing what you want the computer to do by a sequence of steps. And programmers are the professionals who create these instructions, which control computers. These instructions are called programs. Numerous programs exist, and they are developed using different kinds of programming languages. Each language is oriented toward controlling the computer on a different level. There are languages oriented toward the machine level (the lowest)—Assembler, for instance. Others are most useful at the system level (interacting with the operating system), like C. There are also high-level languages used to create application programs. Such languages include C#, Java, C++, PHP, Visual Basic, Python, Ruby, Perl, JavaScript, and others. When a programmer uses C#, he gives commands in high level, like from the position of a general executive in a factory. The instructions given in the form of programs written in C# can access and control almost all computer resources directly or via the operating system.

This book aims to teach you, in addition to the basic knowledge in programming, proper algorithmic thinking, and using basic data structures in programming. Data structures and algorithms are a programmer's most important fundamental skills. If you have a good understanding of them, you will not have any trouble becoming proficient in any software technology, development tool, framework, or API. That is what the most serious software companies rely on when hiring employees. Proof of this are job interviews at large companies like Google and Microsoft that rely exclusively on algorithmic thinking and knowledge of all basic data structures and algorithms.

C# is an excellent choice for developers with moderate to advanced experience with writing code. While experts admit the language is one of the reasonable complexities, they also confirm that it is pretty straightforward, making it simple to grasp and outperform. And since C# is a first-class language, which means it has great readability, and can automate complex tasks that require a lot of time to achieve minor results. Once you are introduced to C# and put in the time to get the hang of it, you can expect to advance quickly from an amateur to an expert.

There are many pieces to understand when building web applications, and chances are it might get a bit blurry the first time founding concepts are brought up. This C# Mastering also makes sure to focus on some additional topics, and if they overlap, hearing the same thing explained two different ways will only make it clearer.

Nevertheless, this book will not teach you how to use the entire .NET platform, how to work with databases, how to develop mobile applications, create window-based graphical user interface (GUI) and rich Internet applications (RIA). You will not learn how to develop complex software applications and systems like Zoom, MS Word or social networks like Facebook, and retail sites like Amazon.com. And no other single book will. These kinds of projects require many years of hard work, experience, and the knowledge in this book is just a great beginning for any future programmer.

Mastering the fundamentals of programming is a crucial task and takes a lot of time. Even if you get incredibly good at it, there is no way that you will learn programming on a good level for a month or two. In order to learn any human skill, you need to read, see, or be shown how it is done and then try doing it yourselves and practice a lot. The same goes for programming—you must read, see, or listen to how it is done, and most importantly, try doing it yourself.

Then you would succeed or you would not and you would try again, until you finally realize you have learned it. Remember that learning is done step by step, consecutively, in series, with a lot of effort and consistency.

Having provided these disclaimers, one might conclude that C# is a great language, and the new features are so original that it will undoubtedly find its place in the developers and IT learning communities. Therefore, if you want to contribute to such movements with enormous growth potential, now is a great time to start. Things are not yet fully established. Many services still need producing, and a small personal project of your own making could considerably help the language community to evolve and strive. You now hold all the information necessary to begin with your creations.

Index

Printed in the United States
by Baker & Taylor Publisher Services